Experiential Learning Exercises
In Social Construction

A Field Book for Creating Change

Robert Cottor

Alan Asher

Judith Levin

Cindy Caplan Weiser

The Institute for Creative Change
Scottsdale, Arizona

Taos Institute Publications
Chagrin Falls, Ohio

EXPERIENTIAL LEARNING EXERCISES IN SOCIAL CONSTRUCTION
A FIELD BOOK FOR CREATING CHANGE

COVER ART: The painting on the front cover is *Waterfall* by Catherine L. Johnson (2004). Catherine is a native of the Twin Cities of Minnesota. Her art has received numerous awards including the prestigious New York City based P.S. 1 International Studio Artists Residency Fellowship and the Bush Foundations Artist Fellowship. In July 2002, Catherine was a finalist for the ten grants annually awarded by the Joan Mitchell Foundation in New York City. Catherine's life has been a journey of overcoming the challenges of significant and lifelong physical difficulties. The first ten years of her life was spent at Schreiner's Hospital in St. Paul, Minnesota and at the Mayo Clinic in Rochester, Minnesota. Catherine's eclectic and artistically integrated life has inspired and informed her art. Her art expresses her bountiful joy of living, her faith in the vitality of creative and healing change and her affirmation of the incredible power of love and relationships in constructing the world in which we live. Reproduced with permission.

FIRST EDITION

Copyright © 2004 by Robert Cottor, Alan Asher, Judith Levin and Cindy Caplan Weiser

Taos Institute Publications
Chagrin Falls, Ohio

Library of Congress Catalog Card Number: 2004104414
ISBN 0-7880-2122-2   PRINTED IN U.S.A.

Introduction to Taos Institute Publications

The Taos Institute is a nonprofit organization dedicated to the development of social constructionist theory and practices for purposes of world benefit. Constructionist theory and practice locate the source of meaning, value and action in communicative relations among people. Chief importance is placed on relational process and its outcomes for the welfare of all. Taos Institute Publications offers contributions to cutting-edge theory and practice in social construction. These books are designed for scholars, practitioners, students and the openly curious. The **Focus Book Series** provides brief introductions and overviews that illuminate theories, concepts and useful practices. The **Books for Professionals Series** provides in-depth works, which focus on recent developments in theory and practice. Books in both series are particularly relevant to social scientists and to practitioners concerned with individual, family, organizational, community and societal change.

Kenneth J. Gergen
President, Board of Directors
The Taos Institute

Taos Institute Board of Directors
Harlene Anderson
David Cooperrider
Robert Cottor
Kenneth J. Gergen
Mary Gergen
Sheila McNamee
Diana Whitney

Taos Institute Publications Editors
Harlene Anderson
Jane Seiling
Jackie Stavros

Executive Director
Dawn Dole

For information about the Taos Institute visit: www.taosinstitute.net

Taos Institute Publications

Focus Book Series

The Appreciative Organization, (2001) by Harlene Anderson, David Cooperrider,
Kenneth J. Gergen, Mary Gergen, Sheila McNamee, and Diana Whitney

Appreciative Leaders: In the Eye of the Beholder, (2001) Edited by Marge Schiller, Bea
Mah Holland, and Deanna Riley

*Experience AI: A Practitioner's Guide to Integrating Appreciative Inquiry and
Experiential Learning*, (2001) by Miriam Ricketts and Jim Willis

Appreciative Sharing of Knowledge, (2004) by Tojo Thatchekery

Social Construction: Entering the Dialogue, (2004) by Kenneth J. Gergen and
Mary Gergen

Books for Professionals Series

SocioDynamic Counselling: A Practical Guide to Meaning Making, (2004)
by R. Vance Peavy

*Experiential Learning Exercises in Social Construction – A Field Book for Creating
Change*, (2004) by Robert Cottor, Alan Asher, Judith Levin, and
Cindy Caplan Weiser

Dialogues About a New Psychology, (2004) by Jan Smedslund

For on-line ordering of books from Taos Institute Publications visit
www.taospub.net or www.taosinstitute.net/publishing/publishing.html

For further information, write or call: 1-888-999-TAOS, 1-440-338-6733,
info@taosinstitute.net or taosinstitutepublishing@alltel.net

Contents

Acknowledgments   vii

Foreword   xi

Reflections   xiii

How to Use This Book   1

Basic Assumptions: Social Construction and Creative Change   5

Learning Labs   19

    Opportunities from Chaos   21

    Change the Context, Change the Meaning   25

    Major Life Changes: Committing to Satisfaction   29

    Social Dissonance, Emotions and Relationships   37

    Change through Appreciation   43

    How to Have Expert Knowledge without the Truth   47

    Mandatory Participation and Creative Change: Can It Be Done?   53

    Gender Myths and Cultural Assumptions   59

    Creating Community: Sharing the Caring   65

    Exploring Spirituality   71

    Death as a Social Construction   77

    Emotions: What Story Do We Want to Live In?   83

An Evolving Understanding of Human Change   91

Glossary   97

Bibliography   107

About the Authors   113

Acknowledgments

This book was born from many collaborations, past and present. The four of us have spent many hours in conversation generating ideas, weaving together strands of earlier theory and shaping the connections between social construction theory and practice. Writing an entire book collaboratively has been energizing and challenging. At the conclusion of the project, there was a tremendous amount of appreciation and respect for one another.

The experiential exercises presented in the book were originally created in the Learning Laboratory at the Institute for Creative Change. It was an awesome experience to examine a retrospective of the Learning Labs created over a 17-year period. Most have been modified from their earlier versions.

Since 1986, many faculty members have participated in the co-creation of these exercises. We would like to acknowledge these individuals for their creativity and their devotion to the Learning Labs at the Institute for Creative Change:

Sharon Cottor, L.C.S.W., Founder

Marcia Cortese, L.M.F.T.

Pepper Davis, L.M.F.T., L.P.C.

Francine Dobkin, L.C.S.W.

Diane Eckstein, L.C.S.W.

Wendy Danto Ellis, L.P.C.

Deana C. Gahn, Ed.D., R.N., C.S.

Edry Naddour Goot, L.P.C.

John Gutierrez, M.B.A., L.C.S.W.

Fran Harris, L.M.F.T.

Lorraine Hedtke, L.C.S.W.

Libby Howell, Ed.D., L.M.F.T.

F. Phillip Irish

James MacKenzie, Ph.D.

Susan Maxwell, Ph.D.

Muriel S. McClellan, Ph.D.

Nancy Olsen, L.M.F.T.

Joe Rachin, L.C.S.W.

Mark Rohde, Ph.D.

Bill Rose, Ph.D.

Rebecca Rubin, L.M.F.T.

Jo Sadalla, L.C.S.W.

We also wish to express our sincere appreciation to the participants who have attended the Learning Labs through these many years of our performing them. We honor their willingness to experiment, their commitment to the process and their feedback about the relevance of the theory to their lives and their professional practices. We have learned with and from our attendees and this has allowed us to add to the richness of the theory.

The Institute for Creative Change has been affiliated with the Taos Institute for many years. Their leadership in the social construction community has inspired us. Our collaborations with the Taos Institute have provided us with many opportunities for mutual, respectful dialogue and challenges. Social construction theory is ever-evolving and these relationships advocate for and ignite new ideas that are integrated into our current thinking. We are especially indebted to Ken and Mary Gergen for encouraging us to write this book and for their continued input over time. Ken reviewed several revisions of the text and offered valuable suggestions that have been incorporated into this final version.

We have had many voices offering suggestions for the editing of the book. We are truly appreciative to Sharon Cottor for her support of this project. She read, reread, offered commentary, created the extensive bibliography and pushed skillfully from the sidelines for the completion of the project. She has been our biggest cheerleader and fan! From the

Institute for Creative Change Faculty and Associates, Diane Eckstein, Fran Harris, Pepper Davis, Rita Boothby and Libby Howell provided extensive feedback on the original draft. We thank them for the time they took reviewing the material and the thoughtfulness of their comments. From the Taos Institute, along with Ken Gergen's devotion to the project, we are indebted to Jane Seiling for her editing in the final stages of the writing. Her attention to detail and suggestions for structure and flow were helpful in solidifying vision and form. Our copy editor, Victoria Hay, provided us with the feedback we have needed to guide us to the end stages of publication. We are also very grateful to Carol Ruttan for the countless hours she has spent transforming the manuscript into a readable form.

We owe a debt of gratitude to our families for their patience with us over these past several years. We have spent significant amounts of time distracted from our home life while we have focused on the creation of this book.

There is excitement in creating, in being creative, in collaborating and in presenting these Learning Labs and their hands-on exercises. For the four of us, there was a synergy to the experience that pushed us forward. Social construction theory is a yoga for the mind that permits us to stretch and gain strength, energy and flexibility in the process of writing. It is our sincere hope that the readers of this book and those who perform these Learning Labs are filled with the same richness of theory and value of experiential learning that has become so invigorating and freeing to the four of us.

Robert Cottor, M.D.

Alan Asher, L.M.F.T.

Judith Levin, M.S., R.N., C.S., N.P.

Cindy Caplan Weiser, L.C.S.W.

Foreword

It is with pleasure, fascination, and a keen sense of anticipation that I have indulged myself in the pages of this book. I have lived the greater part of my professional life as a scholar. I have spent countless hours reading, deliberating, and writing about social construction. The ideas have been enormously powerful for me, opening up new and engaging pathways to relationship, and I have been so very pleased to find such ideas playing an important role in dialogues and development in practices of therapy, organizational development, education, conflict reduction and more. And yet, I have always felt a certain unease about the words I place on paper or deliver to audiences in various climes. The words so often seem to hang there, suspended in air, and without obvious exit into life beyond language. How could the words be vitalized?

Ludwig Wittgenstein helped us to understand that the meaning of language is embedded within practice. To be sure, writing and speaking are themselves, important practices. And yet, if scholarly work is to make a contribution to society, it must be embedded within the broader practices of the culture. And it is thus that I take such delight in what Robert Cottor, Alan Asher, Judith Levin, and Cindy Caplan Weiser treat us to in the present work. First they develop a highly readable approach to social constructionist ideas, and embed these ideas within the unfolding history of the Institute for Creative Change. The pathway is an interesting one indeed, partly in its reflection on recent intellectual history, but also in its tracing the relationship between this history and the deep concerns with societal practice shared by this group.

Most importantly, however, the authors share with us a highly innovative array of experiential learning exercises. These exercises inject continuous shots of adrenalin into the discourse of social construction. We move beyond explication to action; we directly experience the impact of the ideas; we share in the living creation of constructionist worlds. The authors demonstrate how, within a short span, fundamental ideas of meaning-making can be brought to life. In the clearest of terms they give us fresh ways of exploring constructionist implications for our emotional and spiritual life. They furnish innovative experiential means for helping us create change through appreciation, breaking gender myths, and creating a community of caring. And more. As a scholar I am deeply grateful for this contribution, not only for what it adds to the process of learning, but most importantly for its ultimate nourishment of relationship.

Kenneth J. Gergen
Mustin Professor of Psychology
Swarthmore College
President, Board of Directors
The Taos Institute
March 2004

Reflections

The Institute for Creative Change was founded to explore and promote ways to enhance effective human change through a learning forum in which practicing professionals could experience the practical results of focusing change efforts on relationships, human systems and a strong emphasis on the future. Learning how to effectively create preferred or desired change with people and organizations has always attracted those whose passion and livelihood have been committed to generating these changes with those they serve in their professional roles. As relational theories of human behavior and change emerged, the Institute provided a learning community that invited collaborative learning and innovation about a process of change that targeted "betweenness" rather than individual selves.

We at the Institute experimented with many of the developing approaches to generating intentional change that populated the professional landscape during those years when postmodern change practices fired the imagination of creative professionals around the world. We also experimented with practical and effective methods for training other professionals to apply these new approaches constructively and successfully to their own change work with people. These emerging concepts, and the ways of thinking they required, frequently felt strange, confusing and, at times, quite threatening to practitioners who had been primarily schooled in more traditional modernistic change practice thinking and methodologies.

As we encountered these challenges in the training work of our Institute, we quickly recognized that learning the thinking had to happen before learning the professional applications of this thinking could occur. We also discovered that reading, lectures and conversations about postmodern relational approaches to change were just not enough to generate the learning necessary to employ this thinking in our professional work and our everyday lives. This was especially so as our conceptual thinking became increasingly more identified with social construction and the freedom it offered to consciously create our futures. We learned that what was critical for the learning we were promoting at the

Institute was an experiential learning that went far beyond an academic immersion in these very exciting but difficult to comprehend ideas. This experiential learning appeared to fuel the curiosity that we found necessary to expand on an understanding of the concepts and to feel free to experiment with practical applications of these concepts in our professional work with others.

Our learning experiences with social construction and its tremendous power for creating intentional change led to our designing experiential learning exercises of many different kinds. These became the core of our training programs. One of our most successful training ventures has been the Learning Labs that we began offering to a broad professional community nearly 20 years ago. Our development of the Learning Labs reflected our perception that our own continued learning about social constructionism was greatly enhanced when our learning community collaboratively designed learning exercises that would present our thinking and experience with change to others in a structured learning environment. We used real-life situations as the medium in which professionals and other interested people could safely and freely experiment with our ways of thinking. We found we learned more about creative change and we found that others could more easily understand what we were presenting when they could feel it and experience it for themselves within the context of situations with which they were all familiar.

With this process, new meanings about people and change emerge for all involved. The confusion and threat of the new thinking begin to dissolve and its benefits become more evident. Social construction becomes more palpable and understandable when it can be recognized and experienced firsthand in our everyday lives. The relational nature of our human world and all we take for granted in that world becomes more apparent when we can experience it in learning exercises. The freedom of creating new ways of living and relating also becomes more evident in these exercises. These can be very exciting experiences for all involved. The applications are many, diverse, personal, and professional.

This collaborative effort on the part of all of us at the Institute for Creative Change has led to a learning community that we all highly value. We love to share what we are learning about social construction and change and the application of our experiments with it to our professional work and our everyday lives. Three years ago, we decided to put our work with our Learning Labs into writing so others could make use of these learning exercises in their professional and personal lives. We hoped our story would encourage others to explore and promote the powerful potentials for personal, organizational and social change that social constructionism offers us all. This book is the outcome of that decision. We believe that it can provide a guide for new learning that can benefit many beyond our own learning community. We also experienced, while writing this book, what we had learned when creating the Learning Labs it describes; that is, how our learning expands whenever we create a new medium for presenting the concepts and the practical applications of social construction and creative change.

Robert Cottor

I remember the time when Bob and Sharon Cottor had no interest in writing what they were teaching. I think they believed that change was always on the move. How could one ever capture change in print? It's likely to change again. I am not sure what finally brought pen to paper. I imagine their thinking changed after they contributed to a collaborative effort titled *Relational Responsibility*, a book by authors associated with the Taos Institute. Shortly after, our project was born. All these relationships create selves and now we are writers too.

My training with the Cottors first began as a budding clinician some 15 years ago. I would have appreciated a book to help me understand the many concepts we were learning. Our only text was *The Tree of Knowledge*, by Humberto Maturana and Francisco Varela (1987). At the time, I had great difficulty transferring their biological concepts to social living. However, my experiences in Learning Lab, where faculty offered participatory experiential forums, enabled me to learn the social constructionist theory underlying their practice. In Lab, we would experience shifts in perspectives from a dominant discourse to a social construction perspective, offering more possibilities than before. Faculty affectionately refer to Lab as a place in which we can experience *theory in action*, much like our clients will experience when we learn how to think, do and act as social constructionists both in our personal and professional lives. These learning experiences in Lab were so effective in translating a complex theory into an experience that we eventually became convinced of the need to document the manner in which we translated theory into action and, hence, the idea for our book.

Nature is the metaphor I love to use when speaking of change and our process of writing together these past three years. The unfolding of nature is a magical experience and writing this book has been a magical process as well. The seeds of this book were created over the course of 17 years of hands-on Labs written and performed by faculty and practitioners in our learning community. The Labs evolved into chapters and we evolved into a collaborative writing team. We had perturbations to deal with along the natural drift and accepted those challenges as part of the natural process of writing together, remembering theory first and foremost. Nature unfolding is a complex and beautiful dance to witness, and as I reflect, so are we.

Judith Levin

If you are a dedicated Social Constructionist, this field book is a world-class learning experience.

If you are not a dedicated Social Constructionist, there is also a world-class learning experience for you, and you may enjoy the use of this map (there are many maps, and this is just one).

So why would I want to pick up this map and venture into this territory?

It offers an experience in how to expand our ability to make creative, responsible and positive change at home, at work, and in our communities.

Two central geographical features of this book are focused on below:
- Encountering the core **Basic Assumptions** chapter
- The **Learning Lab** section.

I. Trailhead Orientation: Social Construction theory is the equivalent of yoga for the mind. It invites us through different conceptual postures to try on new forms of thinking about how we create our pictures of truth and reality. It invites us to explore how we make meaning in our careers and lives. Social Construction thinking is a skill that, once mastered, allows for the maintenance of an open mind far beyond our previous abilities. An open-minded stance within the continuous process of change in our lives provides distinct advantages for effective solutions.

II. Approaching the Basic Assumptions Chapter: This chapter is a masterpiece distillation of knowledge over 40 years in the making. It is an integration and creation of the best theories, of how we make meaning and thus how we explore the best options for change. For someone new to the understanding of Social Construction, this chapter may well challenge the foundations of how you think about meaning-making and change, but it is worth the anxiety. It is an opportunity to view sacred cows from another angle. Assume this chapter will be a great challenge. Go at your own pace.

An Example: Here is the first sentence under *The Social Construction of Meaning* section: "We assume that meaning, reality, knowledge, truth, values and morals are all socially constructed through our relating to others and our participation in our relevant communities and cultures."

How's that for an opening stretch? No matter what the science, no matter what the absolute truth, no matter what the quality of research, it is the understanding between you and I that will build our version of reality as well as our reaction to it. Between you and I, we construct our reality from an infinity of possible ingredients of meaning, including the realities of hard science.

So why is this such a big deal? Wherever there is an opportunity for dialogue, there is an opportunity to make change. We build our relationships together. If the relationship is in difficulty, has become boring, or needs a good spring cleaning, we have the option to remodel it.

Social Construction Theory is considered a postmodern way of thinking about the world. Modern thought is considered to come from the Age of Enlightenment in the seventeenth and eighteenth centuries, when it was believed there were universal realities that could accurately be identified outside and distinct from the observer. Social Construction cautions that the observed and the observer act on each other.

The right answer is certainly something we all long for. "Just get to the truth." "I asked a simple question, I want a simple answer." "If it ain't broke, don't try to fix it." We all tend to be conservative about change; we believe it takes a lot of energy to change (while ignoring the energy it takes to *not* change), and change can mean uncertainty. Yet for all the yearning for the truth, we all have examples of the failure of the truth, or of the current standard of excellence: the black-and-white legal decision based on *the law* that blocks out the experience of multiple and mutual responsibility, the best scientific medical treatment plan that didn't work when an alternative therapy did, and the negotiation that was successful because all the standard assumptions were tossed out for starters.

Another Example: A mind stretch of yogic proportions in the theory chapter, and this time to the point of anxiety, is a challenge of the concept of individual self. Yes, there is a definable biological felt sense of self we experience. But how do we explain differences in our business self, our family self, our neighborhood self, our sexual self, and our spiritual self?

The chapter says about individuality: "We assume that what we call individual selves is actually a construction of many diverse and overlapping "selves" which are as multiple and complex as the significant relationships and social contexts in which we participate."

There is often fear with this challenge of the one true self, but there's the potential for many responsible and plausible manifestations of self in the dialogues of our relationships. This is an invitation to see how the one self expands into many for great flexibility in response to the world.

III. Steep Grades in the Basic Assumptions Chapter: Anticipate some sore mental muscles, some blistered concepts, some frustration, and some great breakthroughs as you negotiate these steep trails. You will bump into many mind expanders in addition to the examples given above. If you find yourself weary and out of breath trying to integrate all that theory, *take a break and do a Lab*. The theory chapter and the Lab exercises are the two primary driving forces of this book. The theory inspires the Lab, and the Lab allows the direct experience of theory in action.

IV. The Labs, Doing it! There are twelve Lab exercises. Pick one that interests you, and do it with a group at your work, school, church, or in your network. You will have a hands-on transformative experience of this creative meaning-making work. It is infectious. After one good workout, it will be hard to drop this pursuit of contextual understanding of reality as a living, ever-changing process. After doing a Lab, the movement back and forth between theory and application will be easier.

Fire-starting Kit: You need at least one other seed person (an ideal minimum might be four total) to plan the performance of the Lab. In addition, you need at least six participants, so you can break out into small groups many of the Labs require. With a group of ten people, including your seed or starter group, you can experience Social Construction in action.

The small seed or starter group, sometimes formed as a learning community, should read the Lab you have chosen on their own from stem to stern, jotting down notes and questions. Then you need to meet and coordinate your understanding of how you will perform the Lab as you are relationally constructing that process. When you present your Lab, explain to your participants that this is being performed in the spirit of an experiment and an experience. There are no right or wrong answers. Support each other in exploring how meaning is made and how creative change can be generated.

Pausing by the Social Construction Trail, a Moral Challenge: Social Construction has been attacked as relativistic, as lacking a moral compass, as denying fact and truth. A veteran of Social Construction trails knows that to be humble is a good thing. The understanding is not a denial of some absolute truth but an acknowledgement that human biology is not omnipotent. We know that all of us have imperfections of perception and insight. This knowledge pushes us to act in a relationally responsible manner. We should never assume we have a total handle on the truth, but just a little piece of it from our perspective. So we honor all perspectives and try to craft mutual understanding of our living process that keeps the greatest number of voices singing in the chorus of our being.

Alan Asher

Words about writing

This book…

Coming together.

Four. Representing multiple voices.

Honoring history, others, ourselves.

Push, tug, pause, weave.

Invest…time.

Reflect, respect, discuss, create.

Accommodate, assimilate, record.

Relationships, responsibilities, valuing, sustaining.

Play, sort, unfold.

Living theory.

Push, tug, pause, weave.

An invitation…

Proud.

Enjoy!

Cindy Caplan Weiser

How To Use This Book

This field book presents experiential learning exercises based on social construction thinking and understanding that have been developed by the Institute for Creative Change. The exercises and experiences are organized into Learning Labs that promote new learning and innovative thinking for the participants. The Labs are designed both for those familiar with social construction thinking as well as for participants with little or no experience with social construction. The Learning Labs inform and enhance creative change strategies for mental health, organizational development, human resource and community development professionals. They also offer powerful learning experiences in social construction theory and practice for educators from high school through post graduate training. This book will be of value to anyone who is interested in learning how to facilitate creative and responsible change with social groups of any size.

Learning to create effective change with people desiring specific changes in their lives has been a very exciting and stimulating journey for the Institute for Creative Change throughout its existence. Many perspectives and possibilities relating to creating meaningful change have been explored during these years. Many approaches to generating change with diverse populations of people have been studied and tested in real life situations. Additionally, learning effective ways of teaching change practices that appear to work constructively for those seeking change has also been an ongoing process at the Institute, always entwined with the change practices themselves.

This journey of learning, practice and teaching has always been challenging. Working with change is a powerful experience for all involved. The responsibility is awesome and uncertainty is pervasive. New learning and unexpected change is unavoidable. Relational and cognitive flexibility is critical to success. Intellectual honesty is essential. Taking all of this into account, the journey has been immensely rewarding. It has had a profound influence on all of the participants in the Institute, personally, relationally and professionally.

Much has been experienced and learned at the Institute during the years that it has been a learning community dedicated to creative change. It became apparent some time ago that experiential learning with change practices was an extremely valuable teaching tool. As social construction became the underlying worldview and theory of change at the Institute, it became clear that experiential learning was a very powerful teaching tool for this postmodern thinking. Explaining social construction and creative change to others is difficult, often confusing and, at times, incomprehensible. However, being able to demonstrate its concepts and assumptions experientially, to perform them with others, provides a unique and revealing understanding of social construction and creative change. The freedom of thinking and acting generated by this experiential learning is joyous and transformative and gives hope for positive change at all levels of relationship and community in the future.

Since 1986, The Institute for Creative Change has developed and presented more than eighty Learning Labs to practitioners, educators and others interested in social construction and creative change. Labs typically run two hours for ten to fifty participants. Some can be modified for use with large groups of up to 250 participants. Twelve of these Learning Labs have been chosen as a representative sample of experiential learning in social construction. The Labs that are presented demonstrate the excitement of creativity when there is safety to explore new and different perspectives, meanings and possibilities collaboratively with others.

Basic Elements of a Learning Lab:

Learning Labs are designed to produce new thinking about diverse societal and professional issues through the lens of social construction and a commitment to creative change. The primary relational tools used in the Lab are *inquiry, appreciation,* and *dialogue.* Questions that challenge and expand thinking are the oxygen of any Learning Lab. An ideal outcome for the Lab is a sense that the topic is more open to the creation of new meaning and has generated more possibilities for creative action than was so when the Learning Lab began.

Format for Learning Labs:

Purpose: Concise description of the intentions of the Learning Lab, theoretically and practically.

Overview: Brief outline of the Learning Lab's structure and process.

Materials Required: Specific items needed to enact the Lab.

Set-up: Spatial and facility requirements.

Number of Participants: Minimum and maximum number of participants for which the Learning Lab is designed. These are suggestions, not prescriptions. Use them as guides and modify as needed. Size of the group can be adjusted to fit each individual situation.

Number of Facilitators: Number of leaders suggested for successfully guiding the Lab.

Running Time: Approximate time required for completing the Learning Lab (does not include preparation time).

Structure of Exercise: The operating modules of the Lab from introduction to completion, with time lines and description of structure.

Commentary: The theoretical thinking reflected in the exercises. It is designed to stimulate conceptual thinking on the part of the facilitators and to offer suggestions for expanding the group discussions occurring in the Lab.

Applications: Suggests specific types of participants that may especially be benefited by the Learning Lab. It also may seed ideas for creating restructured Labs for different contexts or groups.

How to Use This Book:

It is possible to perform any Learning Lab presented in this book without reading the rest of the book, especially when the reader is familiar with social construction. Each Lab is self-contained and ready to be performed. However, we recommend taking time to read the theory chapter, "Basic Assumptions: Social Construction and Creative Change." It addresses the social construction of meaning, the nature of change, principles of creative change, and the practice of creative change. This is a practical and applied version of social construction that has grown out of collaborative learning experiences in the Institute for Creative Change and the change practices of the Institute's members. The evolution chapter ("An Evolving Understanding of Human Change") describes the social and relational context that has nurtured the development and practice of this theory over the past 40 years. The glossary will provide the reader with definitions of specific concepts presented in the book. The bibliography offers up-to-date resources for those interested in exploring in more detail the many dimensions of social construction theory.

After reading this field book and performing a number of the Learning Labs, readers may be interested in creating their own experiential learning exercises in social construction. The process of inventing a new Lab and then presenting it to others is a rich learning experience. True to theory, there is no "right way" to construct a Learning Lab. Therefore, collaborating with colleagues and co-constructing a Lab to present to others will lead to new perceptions and learning for those who participate.

Basic Assumptions:
Social Construction and Creative Change

We have organized our thinking about how people change into four broad assumptions: The Social Construction of Meaning, the Nature of Change, Principles of Creative Change, and The Practice of Creative Change. Our goal is to describe how our theoretical assumptions and practice guidelines can be put to use in a practical manner. We believe these change practices, which have emerged from our work with change over many years, are applicable to many different areas of professional practice. These include counseling, psychotherapy, coaching, organizational development, management consulting, education and community building. In fact, we believe these assumptions and guidelines apply to all who want to create specific changes in their lives and in their living. It is important to us to articulate our perceptions and assumptions about change in a manner that invites others into an arena of collaborative inquiry and dialogue. We hope to promote an interesting, effective and useful experience with our social constructionist concepts regarding change.

The Social Construction of Meaning

We assume that meaning, reality, knowledge, truth, values and morals are all socially constructed through our relating to others and our participation in our relevant communities and cultures. We are biologically equipped as human beings to act linguistically with each other. However, our ability to develop language and use it effectively arises only through our relational actions with each other. This requires our engaging in linguistic interactions with other human beings. We learn very early to use language to communicate effectively with others, which results in our collaboratively creating meaning with those others who reside in our linguistic world. Meaning-making is an essential human quality. Meaning evolves as people relate together and as their actions and, especially, their languaged communications become increasingly coordinated over time. We believe meaning is created between people within the communities and cultures in which they live, not within an individual person. It does not

5

exist within us, but, rather, exists between us. Meaning is born out of our relationships. We organize meaning into coherent and identifiable constructs that we call reality, knowledge, truth, values, and morals. We also organize our feelings, our meanings of life and our worldviews into coherent and identifiable constructs. These organizations of meaning are socially constructed within the communities contributing to their construction.

Supplementing this assumption about the relational and social construction of all meaning and knowledge is another assumption, constructed within the scientific biological community. This biological assumption is that we are incapable of objectively determining if what we call reality is the same reality perceived and described by others. We believe, based on current biological theory, that our central nervous system is not constructed, nor can it operationally function, to provide us with objective internal representations of what we perceive and experience. Current biological research indicates that our brain is not a camera that can capture and retain external reality with total accuracy. We can negotiate and agree with others that what we are collectively perceiving, whether an object, an experience or a concept, is real. However, we, as human beings, cannot know objective reality with certainty. We are not biologically equipped to do this. We collaboratively create our realities within our relational communities. Therefore, we are incapable of having any privileged access to absolute facts or universal truth, individually or collectively. We cannot escape our biology.

What we can do, relationally and collaboratively, is construct, in language, what we then define as reality and what we agree is true and good. However, the reality we construct socially is a social invention between us, arising from our coordination of actions in language. It is not objective reality. It only exists as our agreed-upon representation of what we think and feel we have experienced. Our biological goal with this relational process is to work together to increase our opportunities for constructing a successful fit between ourselves and the world in which we live. Our social constructions can provide for a "good enough" world, one that can work for us and for our social and ecological communities. Our biological imperative is effective action in the world within which we

6

live, action that will keep us alive and permit us to thrive and procreate. Towards this goal, we are also very capable of changing our social constructions to maintain and enhance our fit with the changing circumstances and conditions we continuously encounter in our lives. We are not locked into one true world, one true self, or one true course of action as we navigate the turbulent waters of everyday living. We are equipped to live within a changing multiverse.

We believe that our ability to create new meaning through relating with one another, within the changing world we experience, presents us with many possibilities for reconstructing our realities and beliefs. We believe that we can then use these new meanings to effectively fit ourselves into changing circumstances and conditions. Meaning changes within all continuing relationships and with every new relationship we form. Meaning also changes as our emotional states change, as our emotional valence and arousal respond to ongoing changes in relational experience and social contexts. Meaning-making, which includes emotioning, is a never-ending, recursive, relational process. We cannot *not* create new meanings over time and, therefore, cannot *not* create new realities, selves, knowledge, and values. We are in continual transformation as we relate in changing ways with those others we encounter as we journey through life and its changing social contexts. Because of this, we believe that the responsibility for giving experiences meaning, for making sense of things, lies within the relationships in which these meanings are being co-created. As with meaning, we believe that the responsibility for the realities and knowledge that are being collaboratively constructed and the actions and feelings that result from these ways of knowing exist between the people participating in these constructions, not inside the individuals. It is a relational process and the responsibility for the meanings constructed between people is embedded in the relationships of those participating in the creation of those meanings.

We assume that our primary vehicles for organizing meaning are the narratives and stories we socially construct to provide ourselves a sense of coherence, meaning, and identity. This process permits us to ground ourselves in a changing and often tumultuous world that can present confusing possibilities, unpredictable risks, unclear courses of action and uncertain futures. Our narratives and stories confer meaning and substance to our experiences as those experiences occur. They tell us how something is related or connected to something or someone else. They provide us with a sense of time and that timing organizes our experiences temporally. They also construct a sense of who we are within our significant and defining communities. Our stories assist us in creating a sense of order, meaningfulness and continuity in the course of our everyday lives and activities.

We sort and select our stories from our recall of the past, from our experiences in the present, from our expectations for the future, and from our many diverse and changing social and cultural contexts. We flexibly include some stories, or parts of stories, and omit others. We integrate these stories and organize them into a whole that we can then experience as a meaningful and coherent narrative. Our stories project us into the future, for they typically anticipate a future reasonably connected to our past and to our present as we currently story that past and present. Our visions and plans for the future help define, or make more likely, the future we desire to experience. They serve as our guide to the future. We also are skilled at fitting unexpected events, situations, and people into our guiding narratives so that we can maintain our sense of coherence and meaningfulness even in the face of events we never imagined would or could happen.

We are both storytellers and story dwellers. We employ our stories to organize our life experiences in a way that coordinates our lives with the lives of those with whom we are significantly interconnected. Our stories are always communal. They are also always emotional. Affect is embedded in all our stories, whether defined as such or not. Our stories provide us a "good-enough" fit in the world as we experience it. Our stories also are extremely powerful in creating our futures. They allow us to anticipate the future with hope, offering us ways of acting with others and within our world that guide our construction of a desirable future. These stories and narratives are evolving social constructions, which are capable of being changed when necessary to better provide for the desired futures of those involved. However, we can treat our stories as fixed in time and static, especially if we believe they represent objective reality and truth. What often is not recognized under these conditions is the great and continual effort necessary to maintain a story or narrative as fixed and forever true against the constant and relentless pull of changing life circumstances and the other inevitable evolutionary forces in our lives. Fundamentally, our story-dwelling is transitional and the new telling of our life stories can create a new dwelling, a more effective fit within the fluidity of our river of life.

We assume that what we call individual selves is actually a construction of many diverse and overlapping "selves" that are as multiple and complex as the significant relationships and social contexts in which we participate. We live in many diverse worlds with many others within the communities and cultures in which we reside and participate. We construct multiple identities to fit these diverse worlds. These identities evolve into our multiple selves. As with all social constructions, there is no true, singular or static self. Self, like all other meaning systems, is an ongoing and evolving relational process. We create an evolving "community of selves." These multiple constructions then permit us to speak with many voices. We become multi-vocal, with our different voices speaking from different perspectives and even different life stories. We can also conduct conversations between our many selves. This conversationally and identity-rich matrix greatly broadens our ability to think and act from many perspectives, including the perspectives of others. This enables us, in a powerful way, to consider and create new possibilities for change. It greatly enhances our ability to be flexible, to maneuver, and to readily change direction when we encounter obstacles to our current life course or serious challenges to our imagined future.

The creation of new meanings is always contingent on past meanings and on the existing knowledge of the people involved, their contexts, and the cultural values and traditions that affect them. While there is no escape from culture, context and biology, the past does not determine the future. Our recall of the past is a social construction made in the present, a recollection of times past as experienced in the present, within whatever the current social context of that remembering may be. Memory is never a mirror of an event or experience in the past. That is not biologically possible. Memory is a story, socially constructed in the present. The past is an edited collection of remembered stories. Like all memories, these are also social constructions of the present. The relentless evolution of meaning continually revises the past while, at the same time, it creates the future.

The Nature of Change

We assume that change is a continuing, evolving process for all human beings and their social organizations of whatever size, form or purpose. We believe change can be sudden or gradual, but also that it is always occurring and always nonlinear. Change cannot *not* occur. We view life as a process of becoming, a continuous process of change, an evolutionary process. All living systems continuously evolve as they attempt to sustain themselves within the environments in which they live. At the same time, those environments themselves are also undergoing evolutionary changes. We, as human beings, are biologically organized to fit ourselves as effectively as possible into the physical and social environments we encounter. However, as we strive for an effective fit, the circumstances, conditions and even the nature of our environments will be changing in response to continuing outside influences as well as to our actions in relation to them. This is a never-ending recursive process that continually challenges us to creatively change ourselves in the service of maintaining our biological fit within the world in which we live.

We further assume that we are biologically relational beings who will, by our nature, coordinate our actions with other human beings and organize ourselves socially as we work at fitting ourselves as effectively as possible to maintain our survival individually, collectively and generationally. We will socially create order and organization out of the complexity, unpredictability and chaos of the world in which we live as we effectively coordinate our actions with one another. This process generates our amazing talent to readily create new meanings through our ability to communicate in language together, which, in turn, powerfully supplements and enhances the order and organization emerging as a consequence of our coordination of physical and emotional interactions.

As meaning-making becomes more differentiated and sophisticated, the power of language and communication overtakes our coordination of physical and emotional actions as the primary source of our incredible capacity to socially construct, deconstruct and reconstruct our selves, our social organizations and the worlds in which we live. At that point, change with people and with their social organizations primarily represents changes in the meanings, in the understandings and in the stories those people have constructed through their life experiences and within their networks of relationships. Change in meaning, which, of course, includes the valence and arousals of emotion embedded in the stories constituted by those meanings, then generates changes in action, including changes in how we relate to others. These changes in relating, in turn, create new opportunities to generate new changes in meaning. This recursive process of meaning-making, change of action, and change in relating is fundamental to our successfully evolving as people living in a rapidly changing world.

Change, wherever it is occurring, may be perceived as more continuous and linear when the increments of change are experienced as small and, therefore, perhaps as inconsequential. However, we believe that change, as a biological and social process, is always discontinuous and nonlinear. It represents a movement or a leap to a new level of order or organization in the changing entity, whether observed individually or within a network of relationships. In addition, in any complex system, and, especially, in living systems constituted by human beings, the exact timing of change, its amplitude and its direction can never be accurately predicted. The future is always uncertain and cannot be predetermined or controlled. If certainty is highly valued within a defining community, then the future can be construed as dangerous and threatening, and attempts will be made to limit and control the future and make it predictable. However, if uncertainty is accepted and acknowledged, then the future can be perceived as providing opportunities for new and more satisfying futures.

Change in any living system, such as an individual or social group, occurs most readily when we are functioning on the border between stability in the system and potentially disintegrative chaos. All of us, within our many networks of relationships and our social organizations, frequently enter this arena of instability and fluctuating meanings. We then either regroup within our existing network or emerge into some new level of relatedness and meaning. When this change occurs, both our social groups as well as we as people change identity. This new level of organization will then be maintained through the coordination of actions of those who constitute the newly created organizational structure at that time, until some new instability is encountered and the change process is repeated.

Coordination of action as a process is intrinsically conservative. It serves to maintain the fit with the world that has been created by those whose actions are being coordinated. When this occurs, it can generate an organizational structure that can seemingly take on a life of its own. This is especially so when a social organization constructs a relatively rigid meaning system, as can often be the case when the organization has been created for ideological purposes or functions. When there is a need for change in an organization or community that has been rigidly constructed by its members, the challenge is to move the community into a domain of relative disequilibrium or disorder, closer to chaos, so that desired change has the opportunity to take place. Qualities such as confusion and uncertainty need to replace the sense of knowing and the feelings of security, control and predictability that characterize stable, relatively unchanging social organizations. The organizational structure must become more complex or unstable before planned or spontaneous change can occur. Major traumas, revolutions and other crises can force change when an organization becomes rigidly stable. However, the cost, in terms of human suffering and the erosion of the social fabric, can be excessively high. There clearly are other more effective and caring ways to provide for desired human change.

Principles of Creative Change

We believe that we, separately or within the context of our social groupings, organizations and communities, can consciously and electively create changes in our lives that represent what we envision and desire for our futures. In our opinion, desired or intentional change can be effectively planned and enacted by us as people at any stage or age and within any defined social grouping in which we actively participate by using the assumptions and constructs we have been describing in this chapter. Change from this perspective is a relational and collaborative process. It builds on the belief that we do possess the knowledge, tools and capacities, individually and collectively, to create a "better" and more preferred future. It is fueled by an appreciation of our successes in the past and present and by our confidence in the future. This requires a willingness to be open to the uncertainties of living and of the future, to find hope and possibility in those uncertainties, and to take the necessary risks to explore new possibilities in the face of undeniable uncertainty. Creating change capitalizes upon the diversity and complexity of our everyday lives and the various perspectives and possibilities, the emerging opportunities, that diversity and complexity continually offer us.

We believe that our primary tools for creating change are the changes we can consciously and electively make in our personal and relational narratives and in the collective stories of our defining social communities. What we define as reality, affect, knowledge, values and morality and what is remembered from the past and expected of the future have been selectively incorporated into the narratives that portray us as people and our social structures and organizations. Our collective stories provide coherence, identity, credibility, and, fundamentally, existence to us as people and to all our social entities. These narratives and stories include the dominant discourses, beliefs, values, conditions, and visions that both represent and constitute our familial, organizational and social cultures. Changing these stories and, as a consequence, the patterns of relationships and relating that they portray, will change how we experience, explain and feel within the new social and physical contexts that emerge through this planned evolutionary process.

Consciously creating desired change requires challenging the status quo, the dominant stories, the taken-for-granted, and the unstated, both personally and collaboratively with the others involved in the community of change, whether large or small. The process of change may be evolutionary or revolutionary. It may be intended and planned, or it may be forced and unwanted. Whatever this change process may be, we believe meaningful change requires changes that make a difference in the dominant narratives and discourses that represent and constitute us as people within those complex social worlds which we construct and which, recursively, construct us.

We all are members of many different social organizations. That is part of living in our relational, communal world. Our survival is contingent on our relational and community-building effectiveness. Within our social memberships, we form communities or cultures to which all members, whatever their numbers, bring diverse resources, knowledge, values, traditions and expectations for the future. This rich diversity creates a degree of complexity within any social organization from which the future of the social entity, and of its members, can be constructed. This diversity is greatest on the margins of an organization, where members enter and leave, or at those times in the life of an organization when the established order is most perturbed, disrupted or otherwise pushed toward the edge of disintegrative chaos.

Members of all social groups and organizations, whether they recognize it or not, participate in a continual process of transforming old meanings into new meanings. These transformations change the organizing narratives and discourses of the social organization and, simultaneously, those of its members. More stable or rigid groups and their members, through their conservation of existing relational and storied actions, perform changes more slowly or "resistively" than more fluid, flexible and future-oriented groups. Nevertheless, change and transformation is inevitable over time in any given social organization, whether planned or unplanned, intentional or unexpected.

We believe that the rate and ease of change for us as people and for our social groups, organizations and communities relates to the degree of dissatisfaction, instability and uncertainty we are experiencing at the time change is occurring. We further believe that there are certain qualities of human relational behavior and worldview that, when present, promote and enhance intentional change and transformation and, when absent, constrain it. Among these critical qualities for change, individually and collectively, are:

- The recognition of the centrality of relationship and context in the change process
- An appreciation and affirmation of existing strengths, resources and successes
- A basic sense of trust of and respect for others

- A willingness while involved in the process of change to cooperate and collaborate with others during defining moments and within defining communities

- A sense of relational responsibility (that is, a sensitivity and attentiveness to relationships as the primary unit of responsibility for whatever actions are being taken)

- The concomitant absence of the proclivity for blaming and shaming others for what has happened

- A strong belief that the past does not determine the future

- An acceptance that memories are constantly being revised

- A comfort with uncertainty and a willingness to imagine the unknown

- A confident and conscious orientation toward the future

We strongly believe that relationships clearly take priority as the focus of change. Our human change processes, planned or unplanned, occur between us as people. Change, like all meaning-making, is constructed socially. We change in response to changes in our relationships, changes in our meaning systems (cognitive and affective), and changes in our social affiliations and organizations.

The Practice of Creative Change

We assume that intentional change with people and their social groups can be supported, promoted and achieved through a focused, imaginative, relationally sensitive form of inquiry and dialogue. We use this approach to generate alternative ways of understanding, to obtain different and novel perspectives and to promote innovative thinking, new understanding, and alternate ways of feeling. We further assume that this creative process, when positively, respectfully and collaboratively performed by all participants in the change process, both change practitioners and those seeking change, can open new possibilities and opportunities for effective action for those who are seeking new futures.

We acknowledge that change work, as we live and practice it, encompasses more than just inquiry and dialogue. Even though language and social discourses dominate our relational activities and actions, more than this is involved in our communication and meaning-making with others. Changes in any of our stories that represent any significant change of meaning are brought forth by all our relational activities within the community defined by the specific story, not just through a different telling of the story. These activities include our emotional communication with one another as well as the actions we take and our physical and emotional reactions within our relevant social context. Also, our assumptions about and expectations for the near and longer-term future and our sense of timing are always significant contributors to how we relate to and construct meaning with others.

We strive to take into account these diverse but critical elements of human relating and communicating in the shaping and reshaping of our theoretical constructs and the change work they inform. However, in our practices as change professionals, we do employ language as our primary form of communicative and meaning-making interaction, while acknowledging and respecting the significant role of emotion in how we relate meaningfully to others. We also approach our work with change with the conscious expectation that we can electively and intentionally create and construct those life changes that we seek.

Our inquiry with those seeking change focuses on appreciation, affirmation, imagination, relational responsibility, context and the hopefulness of constructing our desired futures. We view it as a way of creating the future through envisioning new possibilities and embracing change. Rather than privileging and analyzing problems, trauma, the past or personal blame, we focus our inquiry on resources, strengths, values, successes, affirmations and resilience. We openly talk with those with whom we work about our concepts of relationships, meaning-making, and life stories, about our capacities to construct new and desirable futures, and about the freedom these concepts give us to shape and reshape our lives. We "seed" within our inquiry and dialogue our assumptions about change and the change process. We challenge the taken-for-granted so that we can become free of the restraints on change imposed by conventional and traditional thinking. We believe this approach can energize our hopes for and confidence in the future, a future that we can consciously and actively construct together even though we can never be certain what specific directions our constructions may go. However, with our freedom to reconstruct the future, we can continually influence the direction in which that future is evolving. Our challenge is to move from where we are to where we want to be, through a relational, appreciative, imaginative and collaborative process that can provide many options for change.

Our change practices incorporate five overlapping macroprocesses:
- Defining, appreciating and affirming our assets, resources and what works
- Imagining what the possibilities might be
- Respecting the worth and creativity of all involved
- Dialoguing about what could be
- Constructing what we envision for the future

Drawing on our theoretical constructs and assumptions about how people and their social institutions change, we have learned to perform certain relational moves during the course of our collaborative change work that appear to promote and enhance desired outcomes. The following are representative of those relational moves:
- Defining and punctuating multiple voices, multiple selves, multiple stories, and multiple realities
- Collaborating with those with whom we work in exploring alternative perceptions, understandings, visions and possibilities and in the resulting construction of new meaning and effective action
- Affirming the creativity of those participating in the conversation for change
- Viewing responsibility as relational and recursive
- Recognizing and effectively using the relational and emergent nature of change and the contextual and cultural relativity of meaning
- Identifying "we" rather than "I" as the basic unit of being human and of creating change

- Employing curiosity as a creative force for change

- Valuing the experience and knowledge of those seeking change, what has been accomplished, and what has worked and does work in creating or fostering desired or preferred change

- Appreciating, affirming and emphasizing the existing resilience, strengths, competencies, resources, and successes of those seeking change

- Reframing threats, problems, trauma and crises as challenges and opportunities for change

- Questioning and challenging the taken-for-granted

- Approaching the past as a story open to new meaning

- Focusing on the future and on its many possibilities and opportunities

- Imagining preferred scenarios for the future

- Affirming and employing the power of diverse perspectives and of dialogue and collaboration in constructing possible scenarios for the future

- Keeping more possibilities for the future open by asking what else might work and not just replacing the existing story with the next story told

- Developing creative tension between the perceived realities of today and the preferred outcomes for the future

- Shaping change toward the shared vision

- Welcoming the opportunities offered by uncertainty

- Embracing the freedom that the collaborative construction of the future provides

- Approaching change as an inevitable, evolving, never-ending, generative, and freeing process that creates desirable and satisfying futures

These relational moves are always woven together in our work with change. One is not more important than another. We believe that, when taken together, they create a context for planned, intentional or creative change that substantially increases the probabilities that the imagined or envisioned outcomes can be successfully achieved. The power of these moves lies within their relational impact on those seeking change. We believe the results we experience in our change work are the outcomes of the focused change process described in this chapter.

Learning Labs

Opportunities from Chaos   21

Change the Context, Change the Meaning   25

Major Life Changes: Committing to Satisfaction   29

Social Dissonance, Emotions and Relationships   37

Change through Appreciation   43

How to Have Expert Knowledge without the Truth   47

Mandatory Participation and Creative Change: Can it be Done?   53

Gender Myths and Cultural Assumptions   59

Creating Community: Sharing the Caring   65

Exploring Spirituality   71

Death as a Social Construction   77

Emotions: What Story Do We Want to Live In?   83

Opportunities from Chaos

Purpose:

In this Learning Lab, a dominant discourse that punctuates the negative outcome of chaos is challenged. The Lab offers an experience meant to draw out opportunities for learning and effective action that can occur in the midst of and in the aftermath of chaotic circumstances.

Overview:

Exercises are offered as ways of generating opportunity stories from chaotic circumstances. Participants first deal with a chaotic environment (visual, auditory and tactile stimuli) with little direction from the facilitators. Next, through guided processing by the facilitators, new ways of thinking about the experience are encouraged. The participants are then asked to construct a story of opportunity in their own lives from a story of chaos. Part III offers the large group the opportunity to consider questions that encourage alternative perspectives of the experiences they just had.

Materials Required:

- "Stuff," which could consist of art supplies, miscellaneous kitchen items, office supplies, toys, random items from outdoors, items of clothing, etc. Facilitators use their imagination and bring enough so that groups have the opportunity to "work" with several items
- Table in the middle of the room for "stuff"
- If audio or visual stimulation is to be used to create a chaotic environment, music (CD player, radio, tape player, etc.) or a VCR and projector
- Chairs for all participants

Set-up:

- A room large enough to accommodate "break-out" into small groups and a large circle for the whole group
- Chairs to be placed in no particular order in the room at the beginning

- Table with "stuff" to be in the middle
- Chairs to be moved to dyads by participants for the second exercise
- Chairs to be moved to large circle for final conversation

Number of Participants:
- Minimum 9 (3 groups of 3); maximum 30 (5 groups of 6)

Number of Facilitators:
- One facilitator for each small group. (See Part I)

Running Time:
- One to two hours depending on size of group. Larger groups will require more time for conversation.

Structure of Learning Lab:

Part I

Participants are instructed to divide into groups of 3 to 6 persons per group. Facilitators establish number of groups based on number of participants. No other instructions are given regarding separating into groups.

Participants are instructed to "deal with the stuff" that is in the middle of the room. No other instructions are given.

If music, video stimulation, or both are to be used to enhance the chaotic atmosphere, these are to be turned on at this time. Facilitators leave the room for 15 minutes.

Facilitators return, join groups and initiate conversation using guides below:
- In a few sentences, what did each of you appreciate about the process you just experienced?
- Please share something you appreciated about each person's contribution to the group

- As you heard the appreciations, what would you add that you appreciated about yourself?

Part II

Walk around, mingle and find a partner

- Tell a story to your partner about a "chaotic" time in your life. Take 3 minutes each to do this
- Now tell each other the same story punctuating an opportunity for learning or effective action gained from the experience

Part III

Return to the large group

Large group discussion guided by facilitators to be centered on questions such as:

- How did you experience the questions in the small groups?
- What did you notice about how you think about chaos?
- What surprised you?
- What was your experience of telling and shifting a story of negativity to a story of opportunity from your own life?
- How will you apply what you learned from today in your life?

Commentary:

This Learning Lab demonstrates that meaning and reality are socially constructed. Group members relate to each other, organize their activities together and then collaborate in the construction of alternative meanings. In the first part of this Lab, the groups are challenged with uncertainty (no clear directions), which can be amplified with audio and visual over-stimulation. An assumption in designing this Learning Lab was that participants would experience an environment created in this manner as very chaotic. There is an emphasis on the opportunities that result from the communal negotiation of the uncertainty. The "stuff" in the middle of the room represents resources available for new and creative experiences. One group might decide to take some of the items and create a marching band. Another might organize them by category. Others might spend time exploring or creating a work of art. The "stuff" provides the group the opportunity to construct meaning from "chaos." Roles that emerge in the midst of "chaos" can be examined. One person in a group might observe that she or he took leadership in guiding the group to establish and complete the task. Another person might have felt "taken care of" and appreciative that someone took the lead. The group as a whole might recognize their diverse resources and knowledge and collaboratively offer them to the larger group. Another group might work at minimizing the chaos by turning off the music. Participants also might not have felt themselves to be successful in organizing in the midst of the "chaos." Appreciative questions are used to affirm the many possibilities that chaos can generate and to build the group's confidence of their being able to effectively cope with uncertainty. Simple and powerful Part II of the exercise has participants purposely creating a shift in a story about a "chaotic" time in their lives and noting the experience. In the processing that ensues, conversation can center on the possibilities for managing chaos differently in the future. There also is the recognition that the story we choose to tell guides how we will feel about a given experience.

Applications:

This Learning Lab is applicable to almost any learning context. In a classroom where students are not taking initiative as expected, an instructor could use either exercise to challenge them to consider what opportunities might arise from having to organize themselves with little direction. In instances of extraordinary circumstances, where ingredients for pandemonium can be found, communities can be challenged to look for the stories that describe the opportunities that might be present in the midst of uncertainty and chaos. Examples of these can be found each day in the news, such as terrorist attacks, earthquakes and other natural disasters or a suicide in a school setting. Meetings can be facilitated to encourage dialogue about the stories of opportunity that are often lost in the midst of the turmoil. In work settings, when workers are "stuck" in doing their jobs repetitively and predictably, the company could offer this Learning Lab to challenge them to find ways to co-create a new vision for the future. Or, if employees are offering stories that are punctuating a sense of chaos, they can discover the creative possibilities available to them.

Change the Context, Change the Meaning

Purpose:

This Learning Lab illustrates how meaning is reconstructed when perception or context changes. It is often assumed that our life events can only be told one way, which is defined as the truth, the facts or the reality of those life events. We demonstrate in this Lab how the creation of new meaning occurs when the perception of the context of an event as well as the context itself is changed. This results in the creation of a new story about those events and reveals how more than one story about singular events can and will emerge among those who have attended the events. It also shows how the past can be edited, reinvented and re-storied over time.

Overview:

Three major life events are used as a springboard for exploring how stories can change with a shift in gender, race or ethnicity, socioeconomic status and religion or belief system. Conversation focuses on the outcome of looking at a story about the past from different perspectives and how this approach may be used in constructing the future.

Materials Required:

- Index cards and pencils

Set-up:

- Begin in a large circle for participants to hear introductions and directions

Number of Participants:

- Minimum 10; maximum 100

Number of Facilitators:

- One lead facilitator for large group
- One facilitator for each small group

Running Time:

- Approximately 1 to 2 hours. If the group is larger, more time might be used to consider how stories stay the same, change, or both.

Structure of Learning Lab:

The facilitator gives each person an index card and pencil and asks the group to form smaller groups of four or five participants. The facilitator will ask that each person reflect on three major life events in his or her own life and write them down on the index card (allow 5 to 10 minutes).

The facilitator asks the participants to write numbers 1 through 4 on the other side of the index card and to select as follows (allow 2 to 4 minutes):

1. A different gender than their own
2. A different race or ethnicity than their own
3. A different socioeconomic status than their own
4. A different religion or belief system than their own

The participants are asked to choose one of the three life events identified on the index card and to reflect on how their stories would change and/or remain the same if they had the different gender, race or ethnicity, socioeconomic status or religion/belief system which they have chosen. Suggest to the participants to consider their life stories with each of the different variables. This process will result in five different stories, including the original story, allowing the storyteller to experience the shift in context and the changes in meaning as the story is told and retold with each of the different variables listed (allow 10 to 20 minutes for this reflection).

Allow 45 minutes in small groups to share the stories and discoveries made. If time allows, the participants may return to the large group for discussion about their experiences.

Commentary:

The primary vehicles for organizing meaning are the narratives we socially construct and coordinate with others that inform us and others who we are as people and how we perceive, experience, and describe the world in which we live. This exercise illustrates that who we are is as multiple as the significant relationships in which we participate. We live in the multiple worlds we have constructed within our many relationships. There is no true, autonomous and objective self. We socially construct a community of selves. The creation of new meanings is always contingent on the meaning given to the past by the people involved, their current context, and the cultural values and traditions that influence them. There is no escape from culture or context. However, the past does not determine the future. Even the past is yet to be defined, as can be experienced in this Lab.

Applications:

This Learning Lab can be used in organizational development, coaching, counseling or psychotherapy training to demonstrate to practitioners that their clients have the capacity to tell the stories of past events in situations in different ways depending on the meaning they choose to attach to those events and situations. Understanding how we can edit and reconstruct our histories is an invaluable experience for practitioners and clients alike. It can motivate the practitioner to explore alternative ways of having clients tell their stories and experience the changes in meaning, emotion and behavior those alternative stories can have. These changes, if accepted and assimilated by their clients, can be the building blocks of a new future. The Learning Lab can also be instrumental in education and cultural or diversity trainings by assisting groups of people to learn about the multiple meanings, interpretations and understandings present in any given context.

Major Life Changes: Committing to Satisfaction

Purpose:

This Learning Lab emphasizes the challenge, inevitability and unpredictability of significant change while also punctuating the opportunities for effective action and adaptation that are simultaneously offered during the change experience. The Lab encourages the notion of staying satisfied in the midst of change. Assumptions about the meaning, effect, and consequences of change are explored.

Overview:

The reading of a simple story begins this Learning Lab. The story provides an example of shifts in a belief system as new experiences bring new information. An icebreaker follows involving the co-creation of a story. This serves as a springboard for conversation about change and the experience of not having a preferred story dominate. In the three-part small group exercise, participants are challenged to co-create a plan to adapt to a major, unexpected change. A series of instructions lead participants to collaborate and reflect on their experience. The final meditation is intended to provoke thinking about staying satisfied when change is not planned or preferred.

Materials Required:
- 3- by 5-inch cards
- 4- by 6-inch cards
- Post-it notes (small)
- Pens or pencils for participants
- Copy of story for facilitator to read during the introduction
- Copy of meditation and questions for facilitator to read

Set-up:

- Room(s) large enough to accommodate breaking into small groups and a large circle (preferably) for the whole group
- Chairs set in a large circle to begin the Lab (if possible)

Number of Participants:

- Minimum of 9 (3 groups of 3). Maximum of 30 (6 groups of 5)

Number of Facilitators:

- One lead facilitator for large group
- One facilitator for each small group (See Part I)

Running Time:

- Approximately 2 hours. Discussion periods may be longer which will increase running time.

Structure of Learning Lab:

Introduction

A facilitator reads the following story to participants:

> There once was a man who was a coal miner in a small village. One day, as he was chipping away at a large mountain with his pickaxe, he noticed the monotony of the "chip, chip, chip" sound and he felt dissatisfied. As it happened, it was his day to talk to God and have wishes granted. He said to God, "Why must I be a poor man, a man who must listen to the 'chip, chip, chip' of an axe, day after day?" As he worked and pondered this question, he noticed that the King was visiting his village. The villagers worshipped the King and his riches. The man spoke to God and asked him if he could be King. Within moments, the man felt a crown on his head and robes on his body and he basked in the adulation of the

villagers. He thanked God and continued to wave at the crowd of well-wishers who were greeting him as the King.

Soon, his crown grew heavy and his robes made him feel very warm. He was in awe of the sun's rays and its ability to make him feel so warm. Once again, turning to God, he asked the granting of his wish to become the sun. Soon after, he felt energy coming from him as he warmed the land and caused intense heat.

As he reveled in his newfound powers, he felt a cloud filled with moisture come in front of him. He no longer could spread his warmth and he soon felt frustrated. He once again requested of God that he be changed into something new. He wished to be the water in the cloud and he was granted that wish. He was enjoying the experience of falling from the sky, reaching the earth and nourishing the soil and the people of the lands. At times, the forcefulness of his rain made him feel wonderful. As he fell from the clouds, he felt a mighty force capable of pushing him far and keeping him from his destination. If only he could be the wind! Then, he would feel the control he wanted to feel.

So, once again, his wish was granted and he became the wind. How potent he felt with his new abilities to push and move things and to be free to move about! But, once again, all of a sudden, he bumped into a heavy obstacle he could not penetrate.

It was a large mountain that was mighty and appeared to be the strongest thing he had encountered thus far. He turned to God one last time and made his final request. "Please, God, let me be this mountain as I believe I will feel myself to be the strongest thing in the land!"

So, one last time, God granted his wish and he stood proud and potent. And, as he sat, he heard a sound and felt a twinge. He looked down and saw a small man and he heard the "chip, chip, chip" of the man's axe. (Author unknown)

Icebreaker (a brief beginning exercise):

With participants sitting in a circle, the facilitator begins with these instructions:

> We are going to co-create a story about a major, unexpected change. I will begin the story using the pronoun "I." Each of you will add to the story, speaking from the "I" position, as if it were your own. As each of you finishes your part of the story, please put a post-it note on yourself and pass the rest of the post-it notes to another person, who will then continue the story. The story telling and post-it notes will pass from person to person until everyone has participated. Have fun with this story. Feel free to play.

(This exercise can also be done without post-it notes by going around the circle. If the group is too large, the story can be created using only some participants.)

Following the co-creation of the story, the facilitator poses these questions (and any others that seem relevant at the time) for the group to discuss:

- What were the shifts to the story that were familiar and which ones were unexpected?
- What did you notice about where others took the story?
- What surprised you as you participated in this experience?
- What other observations do you have about the process?

Small Group Exercise Part I

The large group is divided into small groups of between 3 and 5 members. Each group is given a 3- by 5-inch card. The following instructions are given to all:

> As a group, think of a major, unexpected, unplanned or unthinkable experience that someone might have to deal with and write it on the 3- by 5-inch card. You will have 10 minutes to select a specific experience.

Small Group Exercise Part II

Each participant is given a blank 4- by 6-inch card. The lead facilitator collects the 3- by 5-inch cards from each group. She or he gives an individual in each group one of the cards written by another group (one per group).

The facilitator then gives the following instructions:

> What is written on this card has just happened to you. Read it to yourself and pass it to each person in your group. Do not talk. Take a moment to reflect and decide how *you* would like to handle this situation. Write your plan on the 4- by 6-inch card that has been given to you. You will have approximately 10 minutes to record your ideas.

Small Group Exercise Part III

The lead facilitator gives the following instructions:

> Speak with the others in your group about the plans you made to handle the situation. After each person has spoken, please collaborate with other members of your group to create what your group considers the most effective group plan for handling the major, unexpected change.

After approximately 15 minutes, the lead facilitator asks all participants to join the large group.

Large Group Experience Part I

One person from each small group is asked to share with the large group:

> What was the major change the group encountered and what did the group create to handle the change?

Large Group Experience Part II

The facilitator asks the large group to process the experience they have had thus far. Sample questions to encourage conversation could be:

- Was there any conversation in your small groups about whether the "sudden major change" was considered by all group members to be "major"?

33

- What comments do you have about the similarities and differences of creating a plan as an individual and collaborating in a group?
- When or if the major change was positive (e.g. winning the lottery), what kinds of conversations were provoked?
- What stories from your life are pertinent to today's topic? When have you experienced or watched others accommodate to sudden change?
- What do you believe has influenced your ways of responding to sudden change? What were the lessons you learned at those times? (If facilitators are comfortable with social constructionist theory, the wrap-up conversations could punctuate and expand upon the commentary section found at the end of this Lab.)
- Have any patterns emerged in listening to the reporting today?
- For those of you who are therapists, how do your ways of helping others influence your ability to deal with sudden change?

Large Group Closing Meditation

The lead facilitator asks participants to get comfortable and close their eyes. She or he then reads these (or similar) questions as participants silently reflect:

- Think of something current that has changed for you that you have not desired.
- What words would you use to describe your feelings connected to this change?
- What were you expecting that didn't occur?
- What are you doing about the change that is helpful or useful?
- To tell a satisfied story six months from now, what would you want, need or have to be doing today? On what would it be helpful to have your focus?
- Of your significant others, who would first notice that you were satisfied?
- What would they notice?
- How would they respond to you differently when they notice?
- How might they assist you in your commitment to telling a satisfied story?
- At the point in time when you are satisfied, how would you want to be describing yourself?

Commentary:

One of the core beliefs of social construction theory is that change is a continuing, evolving and relational process. However, when change is definitely not wanted, is feared or is experienced as being far beyond expectations, a negative meaning is often ascribed and the change may be labeled as major or even disastrous or tragic. The exercises in this Learning Lab encourage the honoring of diverse voices in the development of a community that will collaborate in planning for a major or highly challenging change. In the small group exercises, with the charge of co-constructing an action plan, participants practice respecting the creativity of those participating in the conversation about possible solutions or courses of action regarding the challenges presented by the major life change faced by the group. The phrase "major life change" is preferred over the labels "threat," "problem" or "crisis." The challenges faced in these exercises are presented as opportunities for shaping effective action. Focusing on the future and its many possibilities can generate hope as well as an adaptive plan for change. The results of this approach can lead to satisfaction even in the midst of undesired or unexpected change.

Applications:

Since change is a continuing process for all people and their social organizations of whatever size, form or purpose, all parts of this Learning Lab can be adapted to almost any context. The exercises offer a way to co-construct meaning about the impact of the change and to plan for accommodating the change. For example, after September 11, 2001, many people came together to tell their stories and plan for a future based on new information and different challenges. Having a baby, getting a promotion that necessitates a move to another state, or inheriting a large sum of money are all examples of changes that challenge a system's existing organization. The questions and exercises can be adapted to any context to encourage the creation of future-focused, creative and pragmatic plans for positive and satisfying adaptation to change.

Social Dissonance, Emotions and Relationships

Purpose:

This Learning Lab explores the difficulty in the coordination of action within a group of people in which someone is behaving in a way that is viewed as socially unacceptable, irresponsible or inappropriate. In the Lab, dissonance is created when a group member's behavior is incongruent with the group's expectations. The emotions generated by this dissonance and the effect on the group relationships are dealt with throughout the Lab.

Overview:

In this Learning Lab, the participants experience the effects of relating in a socially dissonant group context. In an attempt to coordinate their actions within the group, participants are challenged by unexpected, incongruent and distracted behavior exhibited by one member of the group. Participants are encouraged to punctuate those perspectives and themes that promote positive change rather than focus on problems and blame.

Materials Required:

- Preprinted scripts (see below)
- Name tags for each role
- Questions printed for each participant or group
- Chairs that can be moved in the room

Set-up:

- Begin in a large circle for introductions
- The group is then divided into small groups of five or six participants
- One person in each of the small groups is given a script that is different from the rest of the members in that group. A Walkman can be used in place of the different script.
- Each small group may be labeled the same or each may be labeled differently, depending on the desired context to be explored; that is, family, business and couple relationship (review suggested scripts for labeling groups).

37

Number of Participants:

- 15 to 100 participants as the room allows

Number of Facilitators:

- One lead facilitator for large group
- One facilitator for each small group

Running Time:

- Approximately 2 hours

Structure of Learning Lab:

In the large group, the participants will be asked to think for a few moments about the last time they were in a highly charged emotional scenario. This scenario can be a brief encounter or a major situation at home, at work or elsewhere in life. While reflecting on the scenario the participants are asked to consider the following questions (allow 10 to 15 minutes):

- When you were experiencing the "rub" of the emotionally charged situation and were faced with a choice or decision, did you find it more effective to think about how your decision would impact and affect you, or did you tend to consider the possible effects of your decision upon the others involved in the situation?
- Was it more helpful for you to focus on the cause of the dissonance or on ways of moving beyond the dissonance?
- What are the opportunities as well as the challenges that are available when we experience the dissonance of emotionally charged situations?
- In emotionally charged situations, statements are made that invite others to respond. What sorts of statements invite future possibilities, and which of the statements are more likely to invite an escalation of conflict?

The participants will be invited to form small groups of 4 to 6 people. Each group will be assigned a specific identity. The three groups will be labeled *Family Group, Work Group,* and *Group of Partners in a Business.* The facilitator can choose to use one or all of the groups mentioned above. Every participant in each of the groups will be given a name tag identifying him or her as a specific member of the small group.

Members of each group will decide among themselves who will represent specific members in the group. For example, in the family group, there may be a mother, or a father, daughters, sons, a grandparent, a cousin, etc. Group members are instructed to interact with each other as they create the stories of their group.

One person from each group will be asked by the facilitator to leave the group for a moment; the facilitator will instruct the selected person to assume a particular role. The other group members will be instructed to continue their conversation in developing who they are and how their relationships work. The participant who was removed from the group will be given a script and will be instructed to be as fully absorbed as possible in this new script. This participant will then return to his or her group.

Family Group Member Script

Last night with you was indescribably wonderful. Our walk along the deserted beach was so intimate and romantic. I still tingle when I think of how close we felt, how warm and content we were. I can still hear the waves crashing and smell the salt air. The breeze was delicious. When I'm with you, it's as if I have traveled to a perfect place: no have-to's, no deadlines, no worries. When we're together I feel at peace, valued, and loved. We never disagree; we always have fun and enjoy ourselves and one another. It's always good when we're together. I just can't get enough of you. The next time can never be soon enough.

Work Group Member Script

I can't believe how well I did in Vegas last weekend! I've really moved into the ranks of the high-rollers. A comp deluxe room and everything. It really feels great to have the pit bosses recognize me and treat me so well. They bend over backwards for me. If this keeps up, they'll be flying me up there for free on a junket! I can't wait till next weekend, so I can get out of town and get back to

Vegas. When I'm there I feel like I'm on top of the world! I love the challenge of playing the odds and actually winning. I even found this great website that helps me to perfect my skills. I just love spending time on it preparing for next weekend.

Business Partner Group Member Script

What a great lunch I had with the other firm yesterday. What a great bunch of guys! It was wonderful to hear all the flattering things they said about me. And what about that offer they made me to leave this firm? Wow! Their offices are so lush and they even showed me the office I would have. I can still see the fabulous view of the city from what would be my window. I'm really looking forward to meeting with them again next week.

Each group will now be given written instructions for planning an event. Members are asked to play their roles, as defined on their name tags (allow 20 to 30 minutes).

Once the event has been planned and time is called, the participants will be instructed to reflect with each other on their experiences and prepare an oral report. They will also be asked to take note of their experiences with the person who read the script that was different from that of the group. The facilitator will give to each small group the following questions and suggestions to assist in the reflection of the experiences:

- What did you notice about group member participation?
- What did you experience when attempting to collaborate and coordinate an event while one person was paying attention to something else? How did this influence the group process?
- What assumptions did you make about what was happening with the person reading the script?
- Have the person with the other script share with the others his/her experiences as a member of this group.
- Have the other members share with the preoccupied group member their experiences being a part of this group.

- In what unique ways did the person with the script interact with the group?
- In what unique ways did the group interact with the person who was distracted?
- Was the use of the script simply an experience for the person who used it, or was it an experience for the whole group? How? (allow 20 to 30 minutes).

During this part of the exercise, the person with the script will be instructed to share his or her preoccupation story. Discussion will be allowed for the next 15 minutes using the following questions to help facilitate the conversations:
- What were your reactions to the person preoccupied with the script?
- What are the stories you can tell about what you just heard, other than the "bad guy" story?
- What are the common themes that emerged? Create a list (examples: trust, secrets, distraction, choices).
- How did you, the person with the script, experience the exercise before and after revealing the script? (allow 10 to 15 minutes).

The small groups will now assemble into a larger group. Each group will report its discoveries to the large group. After each has reported, the facilitator will encourage group discussion. The following questions can be used to stimulate conversation in the large group:
- What were the similarities and differences in each group's discoveries? How did context, role, and the like shift the experiences?
- How were groups similar or different? (Applies only if each small group had a different identity.)
- If the script was a metaphor for an affair or other emotionally charged scenario, how was the exercise similar to or different from your own experiences with such scenarios in your practice or your personal life?
- Continuing with the script as a metaphor for an affair, what is the relationship between the preoccupied person and the script? The preoccupied person and their various "selves"? The preoccupied person and others?
- For what other situations could the script be a metaphor?

- How can the information that was discovered in this exercise be useful to you?
- What new perceptions and meanings will you take away with you today? (allow 30 to 40 minutes).

Commentary:

This Learning Lab illustrates how an emotionally charged scenario, such as an affair or an addiction, contains multiple stories that have been co-constructed by all of those involved. These stories, like all narratives and stories, are relational in origin, revealing the differences of perception, meaning and resulting behavior among those who participate in the performance of the scenario. The Lab demonstrates the difficulty of coordinating action when one member of a relationship or set of relationships is unavailable to appropriately participate in the relationship. Participants are encouraged to explore the complexity of these scenarios and ways of generating constructive inquiry and dialogue that can create new possibilities for effective action for those within the relevant network of relationships. This process may reveal how a situation initially labeled a crisis can be experienced instead as an opportunity. The Learning Lab can also demonstrate the meaning and value of relational responsibility in all significant relationships.

Applications:

This Learning Lab can be used to explore the relational impact created by a sexual affair, by addiction of drugs or alcohol, compulsive gambling or by any other circumstances that generate intense emotion and dissonance in social groups. The Lab is especially useful in coaching, psychotherapy, organizational development and human relations training, as well as in education, administration and community development.

Change through Appreciation

Purpose:

This Learning Lab illustrates how Appreciative Inquiry creates wonder and hope and inspires us to mobilize for change. Capitalizing on that which is valued as positive in the past and present, the Lab explores how appreciative questions and affirmations contribute to effective change in our efforts to create a positive future. This challenges the dominant discourse of medical health care, psychotherapy and organizational change that emphasizes deficits, liabilities and problems and offers problem-saturated solutions. Instead, appreciative inquiry constructs solutions based on hope, strength and resiliency.

Overview:

Participants will initially experience an exercise intended to be playful, as a point from which the conversation may begin. The large group will be divided into small groups of five or six participants. Half of the small groups are then asked questions that invite problems; for example, what didn't work for you in this exercise? The other half of the small groups are asked to comment about their experience in an appreciative manner: for example, what did you like about your experience? The contrast between appreciative inquiry and inquiry from other perspectives is experienced and discussed throughout the various exercises in this Learning Lab. In the small group setting, participants will have the opportunity of creating, practicing, and experiencing appreciative questions.

Materials Required:
- Chairs
- Paper and pencils
- Guidelines for asking appreciative questions for each small group
- Balls or koosh balls
- Name tags

Set-up:
- Chairs and space enough for participants expected
- Circles of chairs are preferable

Number of Participants:

- 10 to 50

Number of Facilitators:

- One lead facilitator for large group
- One facilitator for each small group

Running Time:

- Two hours

Structure of Learning Lab:

The participants are asked to introduce themselves. They will then be directed into circles of no larger than 20. The lead facilitator will explain to the participants that when a ball is tossed to them, calling their name, they are to catch the ball and do the same to another participant on the other side of the circle. The groups are directed to continue to repeat this pattern, naming the receiver as they pick up the speed, and possibly to introduce another ball into the same process.

After the 15-minute period of ball throwing, participants are asked to stop what they are doing and divide into small groups of five or six. Half of the groups will have a facilitator who will address the group with appreciative questions about the experience. In the other half, a facilitator will address the group in a problem-focused manner. Examples of appreciative questions are: What did you appreciate or like about this exercise? What did you learn from it? How can we build on it? How did the group come together around this task? Examples of less appreciative questions are: What were the problems with this exercise? What was missing? How long did you feel uncomfortable with this exercise? (allow 15 to 20 minutes).

The participants return to the large group, where the discussion continues with the opportunity to compare and contrast experiences (allow 15 to 20 minutes).

44

Facilitators and participants will then role-play an interview, demonstrating how appreciative questions compare to questions from other approaches, such as client-centered, cognitive or psychoanalytical (allow 15 to 20 minutes).

The participants are directed once again to form smaller groups to practice developing appreciative questions that can continue the interview when the large group reconvenes. Guidelines for asking appreciative questions will be given to each small group (allow 20 to 30 minutes).

- Ask open-ended questions that leave room or open space for more than one possibility.
- Ask questions in the affirmative.
- Ask future-oriented questions when possible.
- When asking about the past, ask only about effective action or positive outcomes.
- Avoid words that label or define, such as "problem," "manipulative."
- Abandon assumptions of certainty, as if we know the meaning of what the other is talking about.
- Wonder about the stories you don't know, and remain curious.
- Acknowledge your own limitations in understanding.
- Work to make space for differences in meanings and experiences.
- Recognize when you are in "your head," and not working to be in "their head."
- Look for the constructive and positive connections and relationships between people and things.
- Remember that appreciative questions are based on a respect for all persons, present or not.

Participants will now return to the large group to resume the interview with their new questions. They will then discuss their experiences of formulating appreciative questions and the shifts they noted during the interview process (allow 30 minutes).

Commentary:

David Cooperrider, who developed Appreciative Inquiry as a method for creating organizational change, wrote, "We have reached the end of problem solving as a mode of inquiry capable of inspiring, mobilizing and sustaining human system change." Dr. Cooperrider's comments about change emphasize that the dominant discourse regarding change, which focuses on problems, deficits and linear action plans, is no longer effective in creating change under complex conditions. In pursuit of greater effectiveness, a social constructionist practitioner will see his or her goal as rebuilding hope and invigorating creativity by using inquiry and dialogue that focuses on assets, strengths, and resiliencies while it honors those actions that have been effective in the past and may bring desired change in the future. Appreciative and affirmative inquiry generates a positive, hopeful, and even passionate energy that can fuel imaginative envisioning of the future and lead to effective, satisfying systems and personal change.

Applications:

This Learning Lab can be effectively used in the training of all professionals who seek to be skilled with interviewing for change, effective with problem and conflict resolution and responsible for developing the visions and strategies for any group's future. This includes coaches, psychotherapists, organizational development practitioners, human relations professionals, educators, and community leaders.

How to Have Expert Knowledge without the Truth

Purpose:

This Learning Lab is intended to challenge the concept of a "truth" or "fact" as existing independently of those who participate in its construction. The Lab demonstrates the power of telling multiple stories, allows for the practice of examining bias, and highlights the value of creating diverse perspectives.

Overview:

An article from a newspaper is used as a springboard for questioning conversation and collaboration. The article is examined and deconstructed through a series of shifts in contexts and through questioning. The original news story changes and evolves and the focus shifts to the future and its many options. Five small groups are created to process the story from their unique perspectives. The small groups reform in the large group and are challenged to collaboratively construct a new article. This allows for new, emerging hypotheses about the "truth" of the article.

Materials Required:

- A news article (an example is given below)
- Copies of the article for each participant
- Name tags or signs with identified "characters" selected from the article
- Signs to be used to identify groups (for Part I and Part III)
- Paper and pencils for note taking
- Blackboard, white board or poster paper plus appropriate markers

Set-up:

- A room large enough to accommodate "break-out" into small groups.
- Begin in a large circle for participants to hear the introduction and directions.
- Take chairs to small groups when instructed.

Number of Participants:

- 15 to 20

Number of Facilitators:

- One lead facilitator for large group
- One facilitator for each small group

Running Time:

- One to two hours; may be modified by using only parts of the exercise

Structure of Learning Lab:

Part I

The facilitator reads the article and distributes copies to all participants. This article originally appeared in the *Arizona Republic* on January 16, 1996.

> PORT-AU-PRINCE, Haiti: Residents of a remote fishing village bludgeoned to death five people they claimed were sorcerers responsible for several recent deaths, police said Tuesday. The dawn attack took place Monday in the village of Corail. Police from the nearby town of Jeremie arrived after the mob had already killed the five people, police investigator Max Harry Isaac said. Before the attack, villagers were locking themselves into their houses and bolting doors and windows after sunset to prevent evil spirits from entering.

Participants then divide into five groups. One facilitator joins each group and will represent his or her group as a spokesperson when asked to report to the larger group. The five groups are as follows:

1. Villagers not directly responsible for the killings
2. Mob of bludgeoners
3. Group of dead people: Alleged sorcerers
4. Police
5. Evil spirits

Each group is asked to determine what happened from the perspective of the group's identity. Group members are asked to reach a consensus and construct one group story.

Part II

The participants stay in their groups. Facilitators from each group are asked to share their groups' story with the large group, staying in character. For example, "We are the police and our story about the incident is. . ." After the constructed stories are presented, the five facilitators are asked to leave their groups and place their chairs in the center of the room.

Part III

The small groups remain intact. They will no longer be in their original roles (e.g., villagers, bludgeoners, etc.). They will now represent five "disciplines." These "disciplines" are described and assigned, one to each group, as follows:

- Academy of Metaphysical Sciences (group concerned with abstract thoughts or subjects, such as existence, causality and truth)
- Missionaries (intent on bringing religion to the area)
- Anthropologists (curious about the origins of the area)
- Forensic psychiatrists (investigators of criminal activities and thought)
- "Club Bed" (representatives looking to develop in the area)

The facilitators from the original groups (villagers, bludgeoners, etc.) stay in their roles. They sit in the center of the room, available for questioning by members of the "disciplines."

Discipline groups ("Club Bed" representatives, forensic psychiatrists, etc.) are asked to develop and ask questions of the facilitators. Group members may get out of their seats to approach the facilitators individually to ask questions. Examples of questions:

From a group member of the missionaries:

- What do you think the relationship is between this senseless violence and the moral climate of Corail?

49

- What do you think these crimes say about the value the people of Corail place on human life?

From a group member of "Club Bed":
- Has there been any thinking that the limited economic opportunities in this village may have led to the killings?
- This land is so beautiful. Have village leaders considered inviting contractors to bid on recreational and resort development? Might this not help curb the violence of your young people, giving them jobs and opportunities other than fishing?

After gathering information through their interviewing, group members create a story about what happened in the town from the perspective of their group's discipline.

Part IV

A volunteer from each discipline group is asked to report the group's version of the story told to all the participants. Each group will take a turn sharing its story. All participants can remain in the small groups during this part of the exercise.

Part V

Participants may now abandon their roles and return to the large group, seated in a circle with the lead facilitator.

The lead facilitator explains that participants now must write an article for *TRUTH?* Magazine. The challenge is to commit to a consensus story and to construct the article for this publication.

Participants are asked to volunteer their suggestions for the article. The lead facilitator writes these suggestions on a chalk or white board or poster paper. The large group begins to collaborate and co-create an article. Discussion is free-flowing at this point. As the article comes to a "stuck point" or to its ending, the facilitator shifts to processing the day's experience. For example, she or he might direct the discussion in this way:

- We began the day with the shared assumption that the article we read was a "true accounting," because it was written by a reporter and in a major metropolitan newspaper.
- What have we evolved from this beginning?
- What did you experience?
- What shifting has occurred as you went from role to role, as new information came your way, and as you began to have conversations with others?
- How do the questions invite the stories told?
- How do you explain the story you prefer?
- What questions still linger for you that you would have liked to have asked?
- What will you take from this experience personally or professionally?

Commentary:

As the group participants organize in small groups, they discuss their assignments and begin to create new meanings together. With this process of constructing new stories, the group is challenged to keep the emerging stories fluid and to tolerate the complexity of this experience until their story can be made more simple and clear. As the various meanings, questions and roles shift and evolve, the participants experience the ongoing, relational process of meaning-making. When the group as a whole is asked to create a new article, the participants begin to collaborate in a mutual creation, or co-construction, of another story that incorporates the exploration of alternative interpretations.

Throughout the entire Learning Lab, curiosity and inquiry are emphasized. They generate and shape the creative force of changing visions. Possibilities for new meanings and interpretations are kept open until the directions shift to writing a final article. The concept of creative inquiry is highly valued and is used to generate new possibilities for meaning. The exercises directly challenge us to address any form of media presentation with curiosity rather than with an embrace of a "truth."

Applications:

This Learning Lab invites participants to take advantage of the power of diverse perspectives, dialogue and collaboration in the creation of alternative scenarios. This experience is applicable to almost any learning context involving change practices with individuals, couples, families, workgroups, schools or organizations. The Lab can be applied in the classroom to assist students in recognizing that knowledge, reality and truth are social constructions. An article or story from the current media can be utilized and students would interview each other from multiple perspectives ending with the co-construction of a new article. The Learning Lab can also be a powerful learning experience with any group dealing with the resolution of conflict and disputes, such as homeowners' associations, work teams, and various community groups in which understanding and cooperation are critical for successful functioning. An original story can be presented and respectful inquiry from many relevant perspectives can generate effective dialogue that will create new information and lead to the resolution of the conflict or dispute. This exercise can be adapted to a large audience when breakout rooms are available for small group conversations about the process.

Mandatory Participation and Creative Change: Can it be Done?

Purpose:

In this Learning Lab, participants will experience how change consultants and practitioners can use social constructionist thinking to design productive approaches and programs for specific learning tasks or behavioral change when the participants in these contexts are forced to attend. This approach will include the construction of questions, which assist in opening space for reflection and for changes in meaning as the stories and context change.

Overview:

The Learning Lab begins with a group conversation about mandatory participation in a learning or behavioral change experience. Participants role-play a story involving people forced into counseling by civil authorities. The questions asked by the interviewer invite new thinking and perspectives on the part of participants who have been ordered to attend, and they contribute to creating a more open and generative context conducive to new learning and behavioral change. Other stories in which a person or a group of people are made to participate in learning or behavioral change environments may also be used in this Lab.

Materials Required:
- Name tags for identified characters from the narrative
- Markers and poster board
- Note cards and pencils

Set-up:
- Participants will sit in a circle surrounding the interviewer and role players

Number of Participants:
- 15 to 100

Number of Facilitators:

- One or two lead facilitators, depending on the number of participants

Running Time:

- 75 to 90 minutes

Structure of Learning Lab:

Part I

Begin with brainstorming. Write on a board those situations the group participants can identify from their personal and professional lives in which participation is mandatory, such as court-mandated treatment or a parent or spouse mandated to counseling. Continue with open discussion for about 30 minutes, using the following questions to facilitate this discussion:

- What does mandatory treatment mean to you?
- How does the meaning of mandatory treatment invite you to action?
- What are the goals for mandatory treatment?
- How is mandatory treatment the same as or different than voluntary treatment?
- What could be a metaphor for mandatory treatment?

Part II

Use the following story to role-play an interview with a client who is mandated by the court to see the therapist. Before reading the story select volunteers from the group to play roles during the interviewing process. Select two or three interviewers to ask questions. The interviewers' questions should reflect various ages, ethnic backgrounds, belief systems and/or socioeconomic differences. The following story could be reinvented to suit your audience (allow 40 minutes).

Example Story

Carla is an 18-year-old female with a four-year-old daughter, Mary. She is employed as a waitress and is a student at a local community college. George is a 44-year-old man who is Mary's father and works as a laborer at a local family-owned farm.

When Carla was fourteen, she and her family were involved in a severe automobile accident with subsequent hospitalizations for Carla and other family members. While Carla was in the hospital, she was found to be pregnant. Child Protective Services was contacted because Carla's mother was mentally ill and the unborn child's father, George, was 40 years old.

Carla was placed in the John and Jane Smith foster home, where both foster parents were teachers. Soon after Carla's placement, her foster parents learned that Carla had not attended school regularly and was behind in her education. They worked hard to help her catch up. With her foster parents' help, Carla did extremely well, graduating from high school with a scholarship to the community college. Several months after placement in her foster home, Carla gave birth to Mary, who remained with her and was raised by Carla and her foster parents. When she turned 18, the foster parents assisted Carla in finding and furnishing a very nice apartment in a middle-class neighborhood. She had sufficient income from her job and scholarship to support herself and the baby. The foster parents remained involved and supportive.

On one of the occasions when Carla was visiting with Mr. and Mrs. Smith, she told them she had seen the child's father. The foster parents were upset and notified CPS because they considered George to be a child molester; after all, at age 40 he impregnated Carla, who was 14 at the time.

The case was referred to one of our agencies and assigned to a counselor named Fran. Carla told Fran that she loved her child but also loved the child's father, George. He had taught her many things including how to cook, clean and care for herself. In turn, she had helped him with reading, since he was illiterate. George also expressed his love for Carla and his desire to be with her and to assist with raising their child. The CPS case manager, Scott, at one point contacted the counselor, Fran, and said, "Tell Carla she needs to get her priorities straight in order for Carla to keep Mary." CPS wanted George out of her life.

Part III

Discussion (allow 20 minutes)

The following questions may be used as a guideline for further discussion:

- How do people of power influence the story being told?
- How might the story change when the culture of the characters changes?
- How do our beliefs influence the questions we ask and open or close space for additional inquiry?
- What are the ethical issues in mandated participation? Did your ethical positions change as the story shifted in this discussion?
- Is there such a thing as a neutral question?
- What is the role of therapist, organizational consultant, or teacher in relation to his or her clients or students?
- Are you an agent for your own values, culture, organization or the client/student you represent, or all of those?
- Who is your client in mandated participation? Who decides the goals for that participation?
- Would your original metaphor for mandated participation be the same or different after these exercises?

Commentary:

Exploring the meaning of diverse perspectives of forced participation in a context designed for learning or change reveals the complexity of these situations and the power and ethical dimensions of the special relationships in which the individual's or group's freedom of choice is significantly limited. Deconstructing the stereotypical contexts of these forced situations invites the construction of novel meanings, interpretations and understanding. This can lead to greater mutual respect, appreciation and collaboration and, in turn, can result in more effective learning or behavioral change. This Learning Lab illustrates how suspending judgment and being curious invites greater valuing of cultural differences and of diverse meaning systems. The Lab is useful in demonstrating the strengths and liabilities of various approaches to learning and change that are utilized in contexts of mandated participation. The Lab also demonstrates how gender, racial, ethnic and other cultural biases inform our beliefs and assumptions about others as well as how our questions, roles and context influence and shape diverse outcome in situations which were believed to be predetermined.

Applications:

This Learning Lab can be applied to any educational, mental health, business, community and consultative context in which participants have been ordered or forced against their will to attend a class, counseling session, or meeting. In that context, they are expected to learn new concepts or ideas, to develop new attitudes or change how they feel, or to learn new ways of acting, relating or behaving with others. In the Lab, practitioners can experience ways of conducting inquiry and creating dialogue that can significantly increase the potential of mandated participants joining in and cooperating with the new learning activities. The role-playing exercise can be adapted for any specific learning or behavioral change context in which participation has been forced by those having authority over the attendees.

Gender Myths and Cultural Assumptions

Purpose:

In this Learning Lab, the participants will experience how the meaning of gender in any context or culture is socially constructed and is modified over time through the changing relationships that constitute that context or culture. This Lab also demonstrates how the assumptions regarding gender are maintained or changed with the use of certain labels and their cultural meanings.

Overview:

Participants will be led in a visualization exercise that reflects on their beliefs about gender roles in their lives. The participants will be challenged in the first exercise to co-create multiple possibilities when placed in a problematic situation with others who may have different beliefs about gender roles. Within the context of these relationships, participants will be able to explore how other experiences and relationships have shaped their beliefs over time and to examine their relevance to today's experience.

In the second exercise, the participants will have the opportunity to explore how their beliefs about gender roles can help or hinder relationships. In the exercise of co-creating meanings about gender roles, the participants will experience the implications of their meanings in various contexts.

Materials Required:
- Copy of the gender myths and therapeutic bias questions for each small group
- Copy of the visualization exercise for the Lab facilitator

Set-up:
- Begin in a large circle for introductions
- Take chairs to small groups when instructed

Number of Participants:

- 10 to 50

Number of Facilitators:

- One lead facilitator for large group
- One facilitator for each small group

Running Time:

- One to two hours

Structure of Learning Lab:

Participants begin in the large group. After general introductions, the facilitator will direct the participants to form smaller groups of four or five members. Then the facilitator will start the first exercise, which begins with a visualization reflecting on gender roles in each respective participant's life. Allow 20 to 30 minutes for the following visualization.

Exercise I

Visualization

1. Think back to what you know about the time just prior to your birth. Where were your parents living? Who else lived with them? What season of the year was it? What was the atmosphere in your home-to-be? Did your father have a preference for a boy or a girl? Did your mother have a preference for a boy or girl? How did each of your parents feel about the sex you turned out to be? How do you explain their preferences and feelings?

2. When did you realize you were different from the opposite sex in body, manner or interests? What were the circumstances, the pictures you see of this? Is there a texture? Are there colors, sounds or shapes? How did you feel?

3.   What do you remember about the expectations each of your parents had for you as their child? What impact do you think your gender had on their expectations? How would their expectations have been different if you had been born a boy rather than a girl or a girl rather than a boy?

4.   What roles did your parents and grandparents play in their marriages, their families, their work worlds and their communities? How much do you think being male or female affected each of the choices of roles? What are your assumptions about how each of them felt about their roles?

5.   Think about the activities you preferred at home, in your neighborhood, at school. Were you outdoors or indoors? Were you with others or just by yourself? How do you explain your preferences? How did your mother feel about your choices? How could you tell? How did your father feel about your choices? How did he let you know?

6.   Did there ever come a time when you wished you could be of the other sex? Why was this? What was happening? Who was involved? How old were you then? If you never had this wish or fantasy, how would you explain that?

7.   Think about the books and magazines you read, the movies and plays you saw, the television programs you watched, the news you learned. Who were your favorite female characters, stars, public figures or heroines? What appealed to you about these people? If there were females or males you especially disliked or liked, who were they and why?

Exercise II

The large group is divided into small groups of 4 or 5 members each, and a facilitator is assigned to each group. The facilitator of each group reads the following:

You and a few other unrelated young adult men and women have been shipwrecked uninjured on a tropical island that has no amenities but does have adequate food and fresh water. How much does your gender have to do with your feelings, choices, preferences, and capabilities in this situation? How might your feelings, choices, preferences, and capabilities compare with those of a person of the other gender in this situation? Take the next 20 minutes to discuss this with the members in your group.

The facilitators will invite group members to have conversation about the tropical island visualization. What did they think about what was shared? (allow 5 to 10 minutes).

Exercise III

The facilitators in each small group will begin the conversation about gender myths and assumptions with the assistance of the questions each will be provided. Allow 30 to 40 minutes for this third exercise.

- What assumptions do you make about yourself because of your gender? How do you think these assumptions would be different if you were the other gender?
- What assumptions do you think your female clients make about you because of your gender? In what way would these assumptions about your gender be different for your male clients? What are the similarities and differences between a female and male view?
- If you have strong patriarchal assumptions, how might a female client experience you? How might a male client experience you? What are the gains and losses for both with these patriarchal assumptions?
- If you have a belief that men and women are equal, how might a dual-career couple experience your help with division of labor issues? What are the gains and losses for the wife? What are the gains and losses for the husband? If you have a belief that they are not equal, how might a dual-career couple experience your assistance with division of labor issues? What are the gains and losses for the wife, and what are the gains and losses for the husband?

- If you strongly value characteristics generally ascribed to women, such as connectedness, nurturing and emotionality, how would parents experience your help with childrearing? How could that compare to someone who does not? How could the mother, the father, the male child, or the female child experience these perspectives differently?

- What are your general assumptions when you see a male client for the first time? What are they when you see a female client for the first time? When a couple comes in for the first time, to whom do you talk first? What beginning strategies would you consider for the female? For the male? How are they the same or different?

- Who is most likely to be labeled co-dependent, the male or the female client? What are the gender implications of co-dependency? How can these implications bias your work with people?

In the final part of the Lab, the facilitator will invite everyone to rejoin the large group for further discussion about the process and the conversations that occurred in the small groups.

Commentary:

Knowledge, reality and truth are social constructs created within the relationships of the people participating in the significant communities relevant to any given set of social, scientific or cultural beliefs, assumptions and norms. These socially constructed facts and realities are generated by the relating between the members of the significant communities, emerge primarily in language and are incorporated in the defining narratives and stories of that specific community. The social, scientific and cultural beliefs are then maintained by the communities that created them and they become dominant discourses that are accepted as fact, as normal or as reality. Their origins are forgotten. They remain intact until another competing socially constructed belief, interpretation or explanation displaces them as the accepted norm for their domain of knowledge. This is as true for gender beliefs as it is for scientific facts, theories, and realities. In this Learning Lab, we explore how the meaning of gender changes meaning over time and in various contexts, generating changes in relationships and with those involved in these relationships. As we note changes in meaning, we can also note changes in our relating and behavior within the context of the changes in meaning, such as in our gender-influenced perceptions, assumptions and resulting behaviors.

Applications:

Diversity trainings can benefit from this Learning Lab, which explores how social and cultural beliefs and realities are relationally constructed and how alternative beliefs and realities, different from those of the dominant discourse, can be created. Classroom teachers can use this Lab for adolescents to demonstrate the possibilities of changing meanings, resulting in changes in action. Coaching, counseling and psychotherapy training can use this Lab to practice deconstructing social and cultural beliefs and norms and creating new meanings and realities. These exercises offer change practitioners the opportunity to reflect on the interaction of their own beliefs and assumptions with those of their clients.

Creating Community: Sharing the Caring

Purpose:

When critical events occur that are unexpected and are highly undesirable, events that are called a crisis or a tragedy, people in different contexts can come together in an effort to provide care. Through a series of exercises and conversations, participants in this Learning Lab collaboratively create and coordinate ideas and plans to construct a caring community for a member in crisis.

Overview:

Participants begin this exercise by creating a small community group of five or six members. They are then asked, as a group, to create a plan to assist a person (known to all of them) who is experiencing a tragedy or crisis. When this exercise is completed, the participants in the Learning Lab all join and discuss their experience, using a reflecting team to enhance their understanding of the process of creating a caring community. In the final part of the Lab, personal stories of caring communities are invited from participants to help punctuate the power, collaboration, and creativity of individuals coming together to share the care.

Materials Required:

- Enough facilitators for one to join each small group
- Pre-printed cards with different, predetermined crises on each one, enough for each small group to use (this part of the exercise can be done with a facilitator going to each group and telling the members their crisis scenario)
- If participants are unfamiliar with guidelines for reflecting teams, copies of guidelines can be spoken or passed out to individuals

Set-up:

- Participants begin in a circle (if possible). Chairs will be moved according to instructions in each phase of the exercises.
- A space or room large enough to accommodate "break-out" into smaller groups

Number of Participants:

- 15 to 48 (3 groups of 5, 8 groups of 6)

Number of Facilitators:

- One lead facilitator for large group
- One facilitator for each small group (See Part I)

Running Time:

- Approximately 90 minutes

Structure of Learning Lab:

Part I

Participants begin in large group. They are asked by a lead facilitator to take their chairs, create a group of five or six people, and find a spot to sit as a group. They are given no further instructions about their coming together. A facilitator joins each group.

All participants are told by the lead facilitator: One of the ways that people form communities is in crisis. The members of your group know one another. Someone you all know is going through a crisis. What are you going to do to show your caring?

Each group is then given a piece of paper (or it can be told to the group by the facilitator in each group) that will tell them the crisis they are dealing with. For example: Someone you know has had their house burn down, has cancer, is going through a divorce, has had a child in the family die, has had a spouse commit suicide. The list is to be developed prior to the exercise by the facilitators.

After approximately 15 to 20 minutes, the lead facilitator will interrupt and ask the groups to now have a conversation about what they just experienced in their caring community. They are asked to decide what they would like to report to the larger group:

- What was their plan?

- What were they most proud of or pleased with about their experience in the caring community?
- Allow conversation in small groups for 10 to 15 minutes.

Part II

The lead facilitator asks the groups to come back with their chairs to form a large group. The lead facilitator asks one person from each community group to be part of a reflecting team. A brief explanation of reflecting teams is presented. Chairs are to be set in a large semi-circle facing the rest of the group (fishbowl style). The reflecting team is asked to pay particular attention to what they are "struck with" and what commonalities emerge. A representative from each group is asked to report and share their group experience. After one small group reports, the reflecting team members are invited to share their reflections. This process continues until all groups have shared and the reflecting team has shared their comments.

Suggested guidelines for the reflecting team's functioning:
- Each reflecting team member listens carefully throughout the presentation, meeting or discussion.
- Talk with other reflecting team members about your observations.
- Bear in mind the many different perspectives on the issues discussed. Thus, when speaking, maintain uncertainty; i.e., "Possibly, . . . I wonder, . . . I had the feeling that. . . ."
- Reflections may take the form of dialogue between team members and may include unanswered questions that might "open space."
- Reflect only on what has taken place or has been heard within the conversation that you have just heard. It is important to honor and omit that which participants have chosen not to mention. Make no assumptions.
- Refrain from negative comments and criticism; rather, comment tentatively and appreciatively. Look at strengths, resiliencies, positives.
- Be sure to include (comment upon) each presentation.

- Present and comment on any feelings that the presentations or presenters elicited in you.
- Reflecting team members look at and attend to each other—not those presenting.
- The audience should have the opportunity to converse about what they heard from the reflecting team.

Comments on the reflecting team process:
- "What I describe is what I pay attention to and focus on."
- "Reflecting refers here to the same meaning as the French word 'reflexion' (something heard is taken in, thought over, and the thought is given back) and not the English meaning."
- "The listener is not only a receiver of a story, but also, by being present, an encouragement to the act of constituting one's self."
- "I find myself more and more curious by thinking of the content of all the alternative conversations we could have had."

The large group is asked to "reflect on the reflections" in an open forum. The lead facilitator guides the flow of conversation and determines the length of time to be spent on this part of the exercise. The facilitator can then shift the conversation to a more general discussion of creating this caring community. Suggestions for questions to guide the conversation are:
- What did you notice about what group you joined?
- How did you make the decision to join the group you did?
- What was the group process? How did you coordinate your actions with others?
- What was most helpful?
- What did you learn about sharing the caring and creating communities?
- If you were experiencing this crisis in your life, how do you think you would feel about what the community created as helpful or healing?

Part III

Storytelling

Participants are invited to tell stories about caring communities they have experienced. For example, a Lab participant once shared a story of her niece who needed surgery that would leave her needing physical and emotional assistance for several months. She devised a plan to include a large network of individuals who would agree, in advance, to take on certain caring responsibilities during her healing. It was an elaborate, creative and functional system that allowed her to enter her recuperative period utilizing multiple relationships for multiple tasks.

Wrap-up comments by the facilitators can punctuate the value of sharing communities when faced with challenging circumstances.

Commentary:

This Learning Lab is a simple but rich experience that begins with an imposed crisis and the random formation of groups. Participants organize themselves and are then encouraged to look at their process of coming together. In anticipation of or in reaction to another's crisis, members of this newly formed community create a collective future focused on caring. They begin by collaborating in the construction of a common meaning of the situation they have encountered and then enter the complexity of negotiating relationships and information to generate an action plan. The use of the reflecting team provides experience of appreciative commentary and the value of listening as critical components of community building. The storytelling portion encourages participants to remember and share what can become resources for caring for others. Participants are provoked to imagine new possibilities for sharing the caring in existing or new circumstances. The Learning Lab also demonstrates the meaning and value of relational responsibility in how a community can provide care for those in need.

Applications:

There are many examples of caring communities that one can look to in our present day lives. Not only do people come together through religious groups, schools or families for projects usually labeled as "community service," but we also see the concept of sharing the caring in multiple contexts. The Internet has multiple examples. Chat rooms can become a caring community when focused around a health issue. Petitions signed by caring individuals grow to represent common concerns (for example, Holocaust Remembrance Day). Sites exist where people are invited to visit daily and sponsors then contribute food or mammograms or any variety of support services. Ceremonies can be co-created to bring people together in community and caring. The Learning Lab presented can be used in almost any context to encourage focus on how people can responsibly and effectively organize around a person or group in crisis.

Exploring Spirituality

Purpose:

This Learning Lab addresses the concepts and meanings of spirituality. It looks at spirituality as being constituted by diverse cultural meaning systems that lead to many traditions of belief, interpretation and practice. The Lab explores the ways different traditions present themselves in their stories and practices. It also explores problems that can arise when spiritual systems conflict with each other.

Overview:

The entire Learning Lab takes place in a large group setting. It begins with a brief theoretical presentation on the concept of spirituality as a critical meaning-making system, a life guide. Next, facilitators present stories of diverse spiritual and religious belief systems from traditional or non-traditional origins, which stimulate participants to share their stories of spirituality. The last phase focuses on practical applications of social construction theory when spiritual traditions are in conflict.

Materials Required:

The materials required depend on what spiritual traditions the facilitators want to highlight. About five traditions may be presented as samples. The materials would be the tools of the traditions. For example:

- Native American tradition might be demonstrated by use of a *talking stick* that is passed around the circle and allows only the holder of the stick to speak as the spirit moves him or her;
- Traditions of clothing might be shared as in Muslim and Jewish head coverings;
- The potent power of spiritual drums from many traditions, such as shamanic, African or Hindu, are mesmerizing;
- Many traditions provide powerful and beautiful chants and songs, as in Buddhism, Islam and Christianity;
- Sharing honored texts from holy books is appreciated by many traditions.

71

A number of possibilities present themselves. We suggest that at least one example be nontraditional, for example arts and crafts that are vehicles for spiritual expression but present no doctrine at all except for the beauty of the creation.

Set-up:
- A room large enough to accommodate 30 to 40 people seated in a circle

Number of Participants:
- Minimum of 10, maximum of 40

Number of Facilitators:
- Ideally 5 facilitators for a large group

Running Time:
- About 2 hours

Structure of Learning Lab:
- Introduction of facilitators and participants
- Brief theoretical presentation on the concept of spirituality as a critical meaning-making system presented to the large group

Brief Theoretical Presentation

Cross-culturally, it appears that some sort of organizing concept of "Life's Meaning" is significant to human beings. The essence of the term *spirituality* points to the non-corporal, to beyond the body, to terms like consciousness, spirit and soul. Our self-consciousness and our awareness of our mortality present us with a mystery, a void of understanding that we seem compelled to fill with explanation. It seems that we attempt to make sense of the beginning, the middle and the end. We want meaningful, satisfying stories about birth, puberty, sexuality, parenting, old age and death. Each person's theory, belief, faith and practice form an orienting principle or guide for everyday life. These meaning-making systems form a continuum from traditional religion to deism, mysticism, scientism, and on to atheism. But no matter how different, they are all broadly organizing stories about life's meaning, which in turn guide and inform life actions.

Exercise I

The gifts of meaning and practice in spirituality (allow 60 minutes):

All are seated in a large circle and facilitators present examples of meaning-making stories and practices from a continuum of traditions (see examples in Materials Required). After facilitators have presented their examples, participants are invited to share stories or practices from their own traditions or traditions that interest them. Participants should be made to feel comfortable to share or just observe in this segment. After allowing about 45 minutes for facilitators and participants to share traditions, spend 15 minutes exploring the rich and varied levels of meaning-making that have been brought forth. What are the commonalities from tradition to tradition, what are differences and how do these manifest themselves, such as in cultural and historical contexts or oral versus written traditions? What kind of emphases do different traditions make about the flow of life? Are some, for example, more focused on making meaning of death or more focused on practical life living guidelines?

Exercise II

Working with and understanding spiritual positions that come into conflict with each other (allow 45 minutes):

- All participants are asked to bring forth or comment on difficult issues with spirituality

Facilitators may first seed the process with the following or similar examples:

- An American social dictum says it is unwise and perhaps insensitive in a social gathering to bring up issues of politics or religion. Spirituality is an intensely personal and private issue, and yet it has much influence on the conduct of daily life. Why is it generally taboo to discuss this life-orienting narrative with anyone except close friends, family or spiritual leaders? Is this privacy located mostly in pluralistic secular societies? How does this emphasis on privacy compare with homogeneous societies in which everyone is assumed to be, for example, Catholic or Hindu?

- Spirituality through the ages has been used to justify violence. How can this justification for violence coexist with the general sense that spirituality is peace loving, and forgiving? Why?

- Families are often threatened, sometimes to an extreme, when a member converts to another faith, marries a person of another faith, or questions the family's faith.

- If I believe that my religious practice is *the way and the light* and any alternative is some kind of hell and damnation, and that eternal salvation is a privilege to die for, then it is right that I shun and avoid contact with unbelievers unless I am converting them or fighting them. Is that a logical conclusion? Is it a moral one?

Social constructionist approaches with spiritualities and religions that are in conflict

The following kinds of inquiries and dialogues may be helpful:

- How are the paths the same and different? How can the commonalities be expanded and respect for differences be increased?

- Explore the feared consequences of changing stories. Is the change disorienting, frightening, dangerous? Does it deepen the need to hold on to one's orienting map, to one's steering wheel?

- Future-oriented questions that ask what would new relationships between spiritual communities at odds look like to allow for tolerance.

Where there is grave dialogical conflict or open hostility:

- Look for ways to craft shared experiences that de-emphasize spiritual debate and linguistic tug-of-wars. Shared understanding at a behavioral or emotional level can create experiential bonds that allow for future tolerance of conceptual differences. History is replete with examples of peoples with strong spiritual differences working together in crisis. When there is no crisis to weld us together, a day of working together may be better than a day of talk.

- Other ideas or experiences in these situations?

Commentary:

This Learning Lab explores the role of spirituality within human communities. It demonstrates how meaning is generated by the relationships people form in the process of constructing the overarching stories, traditions and belief systems that guide community values, morals and relational behaviors. The Lab is an example of how social constructionist thinking can respectfully explore meaning systems that are considered infallibly true by their members. Social construction can be criticized as relativistic and as lacking a moral compass by spiritual and philosophical traditions that interpret inquiry about the construction of doctrine as unacceptable. Social construction theory might appear to be receptive to more mystical and inquiring traditions. However, social construction does not hold out for the virtue of any one theory or ideology over another. Social construction thinking is organized by inquiry into how we make meaning and sense of our living and then act on the meanings we create. Social constructionists strive to understand organized meaning systems and their contexts, whether these are conservatively maintained or more fluid. They may also search for commonalities between diverse and apparently competing meaning systems, such as occurs with organized religions, when there might be social value in those competing systems joining in some common cause. The assumption that all meaning systems, even religious ones, are socially constructed enables a social constructionist practitioner to respectfully deconstruct those systems and then assist the members of diverse communities to reconstruct their relationships based on commonalities rather than on negating or competing differences. In addition, social constructionist thinking is not an eternal process of open-ended inquiry without resultant or effective actions. It does support decision-making and a move to action when the most desired or effective action for any particular moment in time is identified and agreed upon by the relevant social community.

Applications:

This Learning Lab can be used for coaching, psychotherapy and human relations training as well as in classroom settings to explore spiritual beliefs and world religions. It also can be expanded and restructured for religious groups that wish to reach out into their communities and find commonality in spiritual experiences. Because the Lab respects differences in religious and spiritual beliefs but also can lead to the recognition of commonalities in values, goals and preferred outcomes, experiences with this Learning Lab can strengthen the fabric of a community by enhancing understanding and cooperation across traditions.

Death as a Social Construction

Purpose:

This Learning Lab examines the concept of death. Cultural, familial and personal belief systems are explored and alternative perspectives are offered through questioning and dialogue. Participants are encouraged to reflect and to listen to others with the goal of understanding how they construct the stories they tell about death, so that they can be more choiceful about what stories they will tell about death in the future.

Overview:

A presentation of different beliefs and practices regarding death begins this Lab. Songs, poems, prayers, rituals and other representations from varied cultural and social contexts are used to initiate thoughtfulness about death. A guided meditation using inquiry then invites participants to discover the stories they have created about their experiences of or anticipation of death. In dyads, an introduction to a significant deceased person offers an opportunity for pairs to remember and practice the art of keeping relationships alive through storytelling. In the ensuing small group conversations, the processing of the preceding storytelling encourages participants to look at the shifts in their belief systems during the exercise. The final large group gathering invites participants to share their experiences and what they would like to bring to their significant relationships.

Materials Required:

- Copies of instructions and question sheet for pairs exercise
- Chairs that can be moved for breakout to pairs and small groups
- Copies of questions for guided meditation for lead facilitator
- Copies of questions for facilitators in small groups

Set-up:

- Begin in large group for first exercise
- Provide a large enough room or break-out areas to allow for pairs and small group conversations

Number of Participants:

- Minimum of 10; maximum of 40

Number of Facilitators:

- One lead facilitator for large group
- One facilitator for each small group (for small group exercise)

Running Time:

- Approximately $2\frac{1}{2}$ hours. Discussion periods can be extended which will increase the running time

Structure of Learning Lab:

Introductory Exercise

For the first 15 to 20 minutes of this Lab, facilitators share stories from diverse beliefs, cultures, or contexts representing different belief systems. This could include prayers, stories, rituals, stories or poems. Some examples might be a story about death from a Native American perspective; Celine Dion's song "Butterfly"; reading of Dylan Thomas' poem "Do Not Go Gentle into That Good Night"; explanation of elephant rituals at the death of a pack member. Five to eight illustrations could be offered.

Meditative Exercise

The group is asked to get comfortable in their space. Eyes may be closed if desired. A facilitator begins by stating, "This exercise is designed as an opportunity to reflect on your meanings of death." Slowly, to allow for reflection, a facilitator then reads the following questions (or similar questions that will enrich the experience for participants). Duration of the guided meditation can be 20 to 30 minutes.

- What are the different words you can think of that we use in our culture for death?
- Take a moment and visualize the word death. Notice what you are feeling.
- Now try to remember when you first heard the word used. How old were you? Where were you? What was happening? Who used the word? What did you think they meant?

- Remember again, how old you were. If you found yourself wanting to assist someone who is this age about a death, what meaning would you hope they would make of the death that is occurring?

- Now think of a time when death was a good or extraordinary experience. What made it a good experience? Who were the significant people in that experience? Why were they significant? What about the experience made it extraordinary? What were the gains from this experience?

- Think of someone who has died who you carry with you now. How do you honor that person?

- How will the deaths that you have known influence your decision regarding dying?

- What rituals have you created or participated in to honor death? In what ways were they useful?

- Take a moment to think about your own death. What meaning do you and your family make of death? If you were to be satisfied with yourself, how would you hope that you prepare for death? What could be some of the "right moments" for your death? How would your life be different if you believed we get to choose when we die? What rituals or beliefs would you hope your significant others would hold at the time of your death? Who do you hope will carry the best of you forward? What do you imagine the benefits could be to those people as the best of you is carried forward? Which stories about your life would you like them to keep telling? Think about one of those stories. How would that story be a gift to you? In what ways would you hope that some of your selves could live on?

- As you think about your view of death, what do you value the most in how you envision it? How does this way of thinking enhance your life now? How does this way of thinking help your significant others?

Pairs Exercise

Participants are asked to pick a partner and find a quiet spot to have a conversation. They are given handouts with the following instructions to guide their conversation:

In pairs, interview one another for about ten minutes each about a person in your life who has been dead for at least five years. Introduce this person to your partner and discuss the following:

- When is it that you notice a connection to this person? Are you alone or with other people? Are there any particular reminders?

- What do you value about this relationship and its connections? How does this contribute to your life?

- What has kept this relationship alive between you and the person who has died? Are there stories, songs, rituals or sayings in particular that remind you of this person and your connection with them?

- If your loved one were here, what might this person appreciate about how your relationship has grown?

- Of the things that have emerged in this exercise, what has surprised you? What has caught your interest? How are you hoping that the connection between you and the person who has died will grow in the next few months or years?

Small Group Discussion

Pairs are asked to form small groups of four to six members. A facilitator joins each small group and offers questions for discussions. Allow 15 to 30 minutes for conversation. Examples of questions for discussion:

- What was provoked by these two experiences (the meditation in the large group and the dialogue with a partner)?

- What was helpful or useful? How?

- How did your thoughts about death shift as the exercises progressed?

- How are your thoughts about death the same and how are they different when you contemplate your own or another person's death?

Large Group Processing

Participants return to the large group. Questions and comments are invited to start the conversation about this topic and about the new information that was generated during the exercises. Facilitators encourage conversation about the opening of space that has occurred as a result of hearing stories, different meanings and new perspectives on death. Conversation should be 30 minutes or more (depending on the size of the group).

Commentary:

This Learning Lab emphasizes that death is not the end of relationships that have been socially constructed. The Lab demonstrates that the meanings, values and practices associated with death and dying are also social constructions that need not focus on loss, tragedy or inconsolable grief. The exercises in the Learning Lab are relational experiences which use inquiry, appreciation and dialogue to invite multiple perspectives on death and dying, positive stories about death and the continuation of relationships after death. The exercises also reveal the importance of storytelling and rituals in remembering and carrying on relationships after someone has died. The opportunity to deconstruct death and dying and to reconstruct it as a transition in relationships can generate a very powerful and freeing experience. This is especially so for those who have believed death is the end of a relationship.

Applications:

This Learning Lab can be applied to any educational, mental health, consultative or community context in which the issue of death and dying is a significant matter, challenge or concern. In addition, this Lab is appropriate for any context in which there is a wish to demonstrate the power of social construction and the intellectual and spiritual freedom it can create when it addresses a subject such as death for which the dominant discourse can be so frightening and confusing. Recognizing that death is truly a social construction and not just the biological event can be freeing and empowering for anyone.

Emotions: What Story Do We Want to Live In?

Purpose:

This Learning Lab explores the role of emotions in human relating. Are emotions meaning-making tools that we create and construct in the context of our living or are they more biological in origin? The Lab addresses how much emotions depend on language and culture to deliver meaning. It explores whether we can share emotions without words in relationship with other mammals. It also looks at how intense emotions change the way we process information and make meaning.

Overview:

A storyteller rotates through several experiences of telling a story to a listener, who maintains a fixed emotional stance. An observer notes the interactions. The listeners model their singular emotion on what researchers now speculate are universal facial expressions of happiness, sadness, fear, anger, disgust and, possibly, surprise (Ekman 1992; Izard 1992). After completing the experiment, the group as a whole is asked to explore what happened and how it felt to tell the story of your weekend to a person who stayed in an angry facial expression and mood. How was it the same or different from telling the story to another listener doing the same with joy? How does the emotional expression of the listener alter the mood or thinking of the storyteller? What is it like to be an observer of this process or to be the listener locked into a particular emotional expression? From here the Learning Lab moves to a didactic presentation of research on emotion to enrich subsequent discussion. The Lab closes with a large group discussion of the information shared and experiences of the participants. The group examines how emotions affect our work and lives.

Materials Required:
- Didactic presentation (included)

Set-up:

- Begin in a large circle for introductions
- Move chairs for small group experience as instructed

Number of Participants:

- 10 to 50

Number of Facilitators:

- One or two facilitators, depending on the number of participants

Running Time:

- One to two hours

Structure of Learning Lab:

Part I (allow 10 minutes)

The Lab begins in a large circle with introductions to include name, family and work context, and participant's current mood or feeling.

Part II (allow 30 minutes)

Divide the large group into small groups of three. Each group then needs to designate a storyteller, a listener (this is the person who maintains a particular expression of face and mood), and an observer.

- Listener Instructions: Listeners are given instructions separately from speakers and observers. The listeners are told to portray happiness, sadness, anger, or fear. They are instructed not to speak but to just exhibit the facial expression and mood. Research suggests that it is rare for a facial expression to be held for longer than four seconds, so ask the listener to focus on the facial expression and its accompanying mood.

- Storyteller and Observer Instructions: The storyteller is asked to talk to the listener about their plans for the weekend. The observer is asked to watch the interaction. The storyteller should continue for about five minutes talking about their weekend plans and anything else that comes to mind. After five minutes the storytellers and observers are asked to move to another listener. Thus, all the storyteller-observer pairs rotate to another listener. This rotation should be repeated about four times depending on the size of the group. It works to repeat the basic four expressions using different listeners, as each listener will provide a unique expression of the emotion.

- End of Exercise Instruction: At the end of this exercise, the storytellers are polled about what emotion they thought the listener was portraying.

Part III (allow 30 minutes)

Large Group Discussion:

- What was it like to experience the different emotions displayed by the listeners?
- How did the speaker's story or thinking change after experiencing the emotional response they got from the listener?
- How difficult was it to maintain the same emotional response? Did it get harder or easier as the exercise was repeated?

Part IV (allow 10 minutes)

Presentation on Readings and Research Regarding Emotion:

The following sources were used to develop this presentation:

Darwin and Facial Expression, Paul Ekman, Academic Press, 1973.

Emotional Intelligence, Daniel Goleman, Bantam Books, 1995.

Molecules of Emotion, Candace B. Pert, Scribner, 1997.

The New Cognitive Neurosciences, Michael Gazzaniga (Ed.), MIT Press, 2000.

A General Theory of Love, Thomas Lewis, Fari Amini, Richard Lannon, Random House, 2000.

Looking for Spinoza: Joy, Sorrow, and the Feeling Brain, Antonio Damasio, Harcourt, 2003.

Emotions, Qualia, and Consciousness, Alfred W. Kaszniak , ed., World Scientific, 2001.

Take your pulse. When you have it, stay with it and make an angry face, and then see what happens to the pulse. A change in the pulse is the signaling of the limbic or emotional brain. It can nearly instantaneously change the functioning of the body.

Basic evolutionary brain structures:

- First, the reptilian brain is an automatic reflex response system, as in fight or flight, eat or be eaten. There is no sense of community protectiveness with reptiles; they don't respond to threats to their young.
- The limbic brain sits atop the reptilian brain. This is the mammalian brain, whose basic characteristics we share with all mammals. This part of the brain contains non-verbal intuitive emotional knowledge that is capable of great power and complexity. The basic emotional display alphabet of the limbic brain as shown in universal facial expressions consists of happiness, sadness, anger, fear, disgust, and (possibly) surprise.
- The limbic or emotional brain is the driver of relationship reactivity for better or worse. If we develop an emotionally positive connection to someone over time, this attitude tends to persist. An emotional aversion to someone tends to stay that way over time.
- Social construction theory has relied heavily on narrative and language systems to describe the essence of human meaning-making in relationships. Emotion may be also described as another shade of language that is created differently from culture to culture and family to family.
- In 2002, Public Broadcasting Service presented a series on the brain that described humans from the perspective of their brains as emotional beings who think versus thinking beings who have emotions. Social construction benefits from exploring the emotional side of meaning-making. It is a difference that makes a difference.

Important considerations about emotion and its impact:

- In 1872, Darwin completed his studies of emotion in human beings and animals. He focused particularly on facial expressions. Facial expression appears to be an extension of the limbic brain.

- The facial expressions for basic emotions appear to be the same from culture to culture, whether literate or not.

- At the same time, emotional display rules vary from culture to culture; that is, in what social context it is permissible to show anger, joy or grief. In this sense, emotional display is modulated by culture and by relationship, a social construction. At the same time, when individuals are taken out of their cultural context and are exposed to a significant emotional loss, there is a universal expression of distress with a 90% correlation.

- Though emotions can be suppressed, the autonomic nervous system still fires signals beneath the surface expression.

- The facial expressions of emotion can be made voluntarily. A child can begin to do this at 18 months. This demonstrates a level of cognitive integration with emotions or the limbic system. Voluntary emotions do not have the same strength as the more automatic responses and the facial expressions tend to be a little off or asymmetrical. At the same time, they can be very effective and convincing.

- Emotional reactions are quicker than neocortex processing. They help people survive when there is not enough time to analyze a situation by contrasting and comparing new data.

- In experiments with rats where the neocortex has been neutralized, the rats are still able to function well using only their limbic brain. Humans are also able to respond and survive without critical thinking.

- For humans, this emotional ability to bypass the neocortex is useful when there is a need to avoid instantaneous danger, but disastrous, for example, when a homeowner pulls a gun in the dark of night to stop what is perceived emotionally to be an intruder and kills a family member. On a less disastrous note, how often do we respond emotionally to a situation only later to think, "I wish I'd said or done that instead?"

- Balance between the limbic and neocortex systems is optimal. With brain damage, where only the neocortex is operational, there is a flat emotional landscape. Decision-making is flawed because the ability to value either positive or negative is gone. In the other direction, where emotion takes charge beyond what is helpful, as in post-traumatic stress disorder, the emotional fight or flight responses to a situation long past may be retriggered by experiences in the present. Those current experiences may cause the limbic system to mirror past trauma in the present.
- Daniel Goleman, author of *Emotional Intelligence,* argues that emotional intelligence may be more important in the navigation of life than intellectual intelligence.

Part V (allow 10 minutes)

Closing Discussion
- What has been your experience when you and others are dealing with intense emotions in a closed environment?
- Do you prefer witnessing a "charged" emotional display versus hearing about emotions? What is your general response to each?
- What is your thinking about people expressing emotion in your personal and work life?
- Did today's experiences affect your thinking about emotions?
- Do we choose emotions?
- How important is it to take emotions into account in the process of creating change?

Commentary:

Social construction may appear to focus on language, communication, and narrative when addressing the creation of meaning in relationships and human organizations and communities. The contribution of emotion to meaning-making has often not been emphasized. Rather, when emotion is addressed in social construction theory, the emphasis is on how it is regulated and managed relationally and socially, which is a social construction. Emotion is described more from a social construction perspective than as the powerful biological component of human relating, meaning-making and communication that it actually is. This Learning Lab explores the contribution of emotion to the meaning-making process. Emotional communication may set the tone of a relationship without a word being spoken. This Lab challenges us to profile the role, impact, and effect of emotion on the outcomes and consequences of the meaning-making process. The concept of the social construction of meaning must take into account all dimensions of our relational actions, behaviors and communications and their ongoing recursive natures in its explanation of how meaning and reality are created in the human community. Language, emotion, and physical actions are woven together into the fabric of all human relating from which meaning and its organizing structure continually evolve. We cannot escape from this human process and context but we can use our knowledge of it to make ourselves freer with our choices and their outcomes in the future.

Applications:

This Learning Lab would be valuable for psychology related classes to experience the complexity of communication, emotion and meaning-making. It could also be used as a sensitization experience for persons working in human service and behavioral and organizational change professions to increase awareness of how language, thinking and emotion impact perception and meaning. All who are interested in effective communication can benefit from the exploration of the powerful emotional drivers of meaning-making in a diverse and complex world.

An Evolving Understanding of Human Change

The underlying theoretical assumptions of the Institute for Creative Change have been evolving throughout the existence of the Institute. The members of the Institute have worked together in a learning community and have intentionally challenged and reorganized their thinking about how people change. The resulting shared understandings have provided a sense of coherence, meaningfulness and productivity in the work of the Institute and in the members' professional and personal lives. The current theoretical assumptions integrate an array of diverse experiences, perceptions and assumptions from the past as well as expectations for the future. These are evolving constructs that have no clear beginnings or endings. It is as if they are the middle of a never-ending story. The attempt to maintain coherence and fit with these constructs over time brings unexpected new twists, successes and failures. These emerging experiences are an invitation to reconsider existing assumptions about change on an ongoing basis.

The Institute's expectation about change anticipates the uncertainty of the future and welcomes the opportunity for novel and unexpected experiences to provide new understandings and previously unrecognized possibilities for effective action in the future. Theories will change and evolve, just as all living things change and evolve, as they maintain their relational and contextual fit in their social and physical environments. The Institute's relevant social context has been and continues to be generating desired intentional change with people, their social systems and their organizations.

Early Beginnings: The 1960s

The story of the Institute's theoretical assumptions begins with the early experiences of Bob and Sharon Cottor, the founders of the Institute, who began to learn about and practice family therapy in the 1960s. They had been questioning the traditional individualistic, deficit-based, and problem-saturated psychological theories and psychotherapy practices dominant in the mental health field at that time and had discovered the work of Virginia Satir and the other pioneers in family therapy at the Mental Research Institute in Palo Alto. While experimenting with family therapy, Bob and Sharon paid increasing attention to the relational and interactive dimensions of the people with whom they worked as they developed a family therapy model for their practices. This early model focused on the various relationships within the family, including the extended family, and the relationship of the family to its social context.

Bob and Sharon found that changes in these relationships, inside and outside the family, led to changes in family members, changes that the clinical traditions at the time considered to be individually determined. They observed that social context had a critical effect on the ways in which people related to others and their ways of behaving in general. Bob and Sharon also observed that neither past histories of the family members nor their diagnosable pathologies necessarily constrained change. They gradually recognized that desired outcomes would occur more readily when an emphasis was placed on existing abilities to change relationship behavior with others and on what family members would like their family to look like in the future. Further, they observed that desired change was more probable when clients were actively and openly engaged in the therapy conversation and felt someone was genuinely listening to them during the therapy process.

Family Therapy and Family Systems: The 1970s

When Bob and Sharon arrived in Phoenix in 1971, family therapy was in its infancy in the local professional community. Variations from dominant mental health theories and practices, including the innovative work of Milton Erickson, M.D., who had lived in Phoenix for years, were discounted by senior practitioners in the community. Bob and Sharon were challenged to represent their style of working in a way that would make it understandable to the referral sources they needed for a successful practice. This challenge pushed them to organize their own thinking into coherent and meaningful constructs that they could effectively share with others. The need to describe their work so that others could understand how they were practicing created for Bob and Sharon an appreciation of how relationships, stories and changes in meaning were critical elements in how people perceived, felt, thought, and acted. They began to recognize the ways in which evolving meanings and stories changed how people behaved as well as how they experienced and defined themselves and others.

As Bob and Sharon functioned as storytellers of their work in their community, new meanings were created through their conversations between themselves and with their clients, friends, and peers. The emerging family systems theories of that era, the concepts of cybernetics, and their experience with Milton Erickson were absorbed into their thinking and practice and into their new ventures in family therapy training with other practicing clinicians. Bob and Sharon's story about theory and practice went through many revisions as it was told during the 1970s and it began to emerge as a social psychology. The evolving relational perspective of how people could create change in their lives informed the early work and theory of the Institute for Creative Change, which Bob and Sharon founded in 1980 as the Postgraduate Institute for Family Therapy. The Institute became a forum for practicing mental health professionals to learn about family systems theory, family therapy, and other innovative practice models at that time.

The Institute for Family Therapy and Open Living Systems: The 1980s

With the creation of the Postgraduate Institute for Family Therapy, the emphasis on learning gradually shifted from learning about therapy to learning about the process of change, from technique to thinking about the role of language in change. The Institute provided an extremely rich relational soil from which the seeds of the 1960s and 1970s grew and developed, creating a way of making sense of change that led to the transformations in theory and practice that represent the Institute for Creative Change today. A driving force in this process has been the continuing desire to describe, demonstrate, and perform the evolving theory and practices, which, in their telling and performance, elicit responses from others that then recursively generate a newer version of the theoretical and practice stories. This coordination of action, which is a relational phenomenon, has been a powerful process, one that can incorporate new information and perturbations of whatever kind as it creates a new sentence, paragraph, or chapter in the story generated by our relatedness.

The accumulating observations of how change in relatedness could be integrated into existing experience as an evolving story with ever-new meanings of reality, values and self had a profound influence on the conceptual thinking of the Institute. Within the Institute, that powerful equation of change in relatedness and change in meaning was observed in the emerging conceptualizations about theory and practice and in the training and the Learning Laboratories the Institute was offering other professionals. It also appeared in the professional practices of the Institute members. This core concept of relatedness and change became the foundation of theory construction at the Institute. It led to an emphasis on learning about relatedness, the role of language and how to create environments of respect, responsibilities, appreciation and dialogue that would enhance effective change.

In the early 1980s, the Institute began to follow the work Karl Tomm was doing at the University of Calgary with the interview protocols created by Mara Selvini Palazzoli, Luigi Boscolo, Gianfranco Cecchin, and Giuliana Prata, an innovative group of psychiatrists and family therapists in Milan, Italy. Using Tomm's work as a guide, the Institute explored the human systems concepts of the Milan group and experimented with their thinking and their inventive questioning and interventions in change practices. The members of the Institute also learned a great deal about Tomm's own thinking and his unique process of questioning. These learning experiences renewed an appreciation of how much freedom with creativity was possible when thinking outside the dominant narratives and traditions of existing psychotherapeutic culture. In addition, the Institute owes a debt of gratitude to Karl Tomm for introducing Humberto Maturana, a Chilean theoretical biologist who became the next major influence in the Institute's understanding of change theory and ways of practicing change work.

Maturana's concepts of structural coupling and coordination of actions in living systems and the evolutionary survival of the fit versus the competitive survival of the "fittest" have been extremely useful in theory building and change work. Also, Maturana's thinking about language and communication, the biological impossibility of knowing reality with certainty, and the opportunity to create a more adaptive fit through effective action have significantly contributed to earlier assumptions about the nature of human change.

Later in the 1980s, the Institute began to explore the new scientific thinking about chaos, far-from-equilibrium systems, order arising out of disorder, and complex adaptive systems that display emergent behavior and how these concepts could fit into existing theoretical constructs and change work practices. The thinking about change inherent in the scientific study of complexity and of self-organizing emergent systems that evolve without a pacemaker or centralized authority proved to be very relevant for relational and social change. These biological and physical science concepts were then integrated into the theoretical concepts of Maturana and our earlier human systems concepts.

The Institute for Creative Change and Social Construction: The 1990s and 2000s
In retrospect, the Institute simultaneously being story tellers and story dwellers and each of these dramatically shaping the other was effective preparation for our most recent transformation. In the 1990s, the challenging and creative ideas of postmodern thinking, and specifically, those of social construction, began to emerge in the mental health and organizational development professional communities. The thinking, the assumptions, and especially the challenges of social construction were quickly assimilated into our theoretical assumptions about change. In 1995, the name of the Institute was changed to the Institute for Creative Change. This reflected the evolving change in theory as well as a concomitant shift in emphasis from psychotherapy to a much broader domain of change with people and their communities. The Institute adopted the umbrella of social construction as a metatheory into which the many diverse strands of our earlier conceptual understandings could be woven coherently. This has permitted the construction of a theory and practice discourse that has generated many new possibilities for even more effective action in the professional practice of change. The Institute is deeply appreciative of the Taos Institute opening the doors to this newest transformation of theory and practice.

The Institute for Creative Change enjoys a close relationship with the Taos Institute and considers its founders to be "ex-officio" members of our learning community. The Institute is indebted to Ken and Mary Gergen, Sheila McNamee, David Cooperrider, Harlene Anderson and Diana Whitney for all we have learned in our multiple relationships with them, both in person and in text. The relational origins of reality and values, the critical nature of "we" as the basic unit of human meaning-making, the emphasis on relational responsibility and the power of appreciative inquiry are representative of the conceptual ideas emanating from their social constructionist thinking that have been integrated into the Institute's current assumptions about change. The courage of the pioneering Taos professionals in challenging the dominant discourses in our social and professional culture has been highly valued by all of us at the Institute for Creative Change. This has paved the way for another revolution in theory and practice that provides a sense of freedom to reconstruct the world in which we live.

Social construction provides an extraordinary context for reintegrating the thinking and experience gained from many innovators and mentors in the past, which includes clients as well as family, friends, peers, and colleagues. The Institute's narrative about change work and the theoretical constructs that both constitute and are constituted by that work is a 40-year representation of social construction in action. It demonstrates an emphasis on reconstruction rather than on deconstruction in relational work. It also demonstrates a simultaneous emphasis on appreciating and affirming collective assets and resources and on using imagination to construct the future. This thinking and these practices work! They generate a form of inquiry and dialogue that reveals formerly unrecognized possibilities for effective action regarding desired visions, goals and outcomes for the future. They generate effective Creative Change.

Glossary

Appreciative Inquiry: A form of organizational intervention developed by David Cooperrider (1990) and his colleagues at Case Western Reserve. Cooperrider claims that within every organization, no matter how embroiled in conflict, one can find success, strength, and beauty. Appreciative Inquiry emphasizes the voices of appreciation to envision a new future. Questions of appreciation are asked about what has been effective, successful, and exciting or stimulating in the past to shift the focus away from problem talk and a reification of the problem. These moments of success and positive feelings are punctuated in the co-construction of the future. Appreciative Inquiry is a method of organizational development in which the emphasis is placed on what the community, organization, or people have done well in the past and are doing well in the present. Participants are asked what factors give life to the organization and when it has been and presently is the most alive, successful and effective. Participants are invited to imagine and design a better future. What are the possibilities, expressed and unexpressed, that provide opportunities for more effective forms of community, organization or relationships? In the process of defining the positive and creating an image of a desirable future, the conflict and divisiveness that had existed in the organization begins to dissolve, loses its power and is replaced by hope for the future.

Both-and: A phrase that permits and emphasizes multiple and contradictory positions at the same time. For example, "I am fearful and I am determined."

Change Practices: The defining characteristic of a change practice is the primary focus on promoting, facilitating, generating, or creating the desired change with those seeking specific change. It emphasizes the collaborative construction of what is envisioned (rather than specific problem solving), repair of deficits, or exploring the past for better understanding. These professional services may include individuals or any size or type of social group, from couples and families to workgroups and companies to institutions and communities.

Change Practitioners: Practitioners who focus primarily on generating desired change for those who seek their services. The emphasis of these practitioners is on the thinking, acting and relating that will provide the desired outcomes. These practitioners do not emphasize exploring or revisiting the past, healing old emotional or social wounds, or solving specific problems. Rather, they seek to envision and create new futures. Their work, if done effectively, can resolve or dissolve issues, deficits and problems from the past or present through a change in context, meaning, and action.

Change Story: One of many possible alternative stories that offer new or different perspectives, thinking and meanings that would change the status quo and create new opportunities for the future. The process of constructing these change stories and the new visions or scenarios created by this process generate the hope, energy, goals and guidelines that give the new vision its power and substance.

Change Work: A descriptive phrase used to punctuate intentional change as the goal and work as the medium for creating the shift in attitude, perception, thinking, and relational behavior required to generate and maintain meaningful life change. Change work is the common denominator in psychotherapy, counseling, coaching, education, community building, and organizational development.

Chaos: A scientific theory seeded in the early 1970s by Edward Lorenz, who wanted to predict long term weather patterns. Through computer models, Lorenz found that weather was a nonlinear system that could never be predicted over the long term. In what then seemed to be chaos, Lorenz did find patterns within disturbances or patterns of orderly disorder. Chaos theory underlines the importance of initial conditions and of small changes on total outcome. Human beings and their relational systems are nonlinear systems. Our meanings and our predictabilities are formed within the context of the complexity of our relationships. A linear system, such as a lock and a key, is very predictable—at least until the lock and key begin to wear out. Chaos theory points out that, even in the hardest of sciences, we deal with approximations and context-driven meanings.

Collaborative Outcome: A term that describes working collectively and cooperatively toward mutual goals and visions for the future. The meanings that are created within all the relationships involved in the collaborative effort and the resulting actions are coordinated in the seeking of possible solutions. Even a single person, with his or her various voices and selves, can act collaboratively when that person takes those multiple voices, relevant relationships and context into account as he or she makes and takes action.

Community of Selves: This metaphor is representative of the interaction and interrelationship of the multiple selves that dwell within a person. The traditional concept of an integrated individual self is seen as inaccurate and limiting and is replaced with a belief that each person interacts relationally with his or her numerous "selves." The notion of a community of selves describes the ongoing processes of relating what happens between these "selves," propelling a person to think, act, and relate in specific ways. A similar metaphor would be a chorus of voices, all of which you have made your own. The community of selves works in concert to advise, challenge, guide, move and create different sounds and music to present to the world.

Conservation: A term describing Humberto Maturana's observation that biological organisms tend to maintain patterns of behavior and relating to others within their given environment unless perturbed by the environment or others in that environment to change. There is always a tendency in nature to conserve form and function and resist generating change, at least as long as there continues to be an adaptive fit for the organism.

Constructing: A metaphor for and a description of the process of creating or generating new meanings, stories and behaviors within a specified group of people. It applies to ideas, thinking, explanations, emotion, realities, truth, values, and morals as well as the creation of new or changed relationships in social contexts and organizations of all kinds and sizes.

Constructing the Future: A description of how a desired future can be created effectively through a process of inquiry and dialogue between the relevant parties in any given social system. This process permits and promotes the evolution of meanings, values and a myriad of social behaviors that can be shaped in the directions we prefer. With imagination and our capacity to invent many possibilities for the future, we can construct purposeful change through the fluidity of our most powerful relational tool, our ability to create stories that then reinvent our lives together.

Coordination of Actions: The process by which people organize themselves individually and socially as they relate, communicate and make meaning together. Through recurrent and recursive interactions, an alignment of thinking, behavior and functioning is organized and reorganized over time as our social context changes. This is a continuous process that may be experienced as smooth or as turbulent at any given time.

Deconstructing: The process of taking apart a story or idea to examine how it came to be and how particular meanings resulted from that specific telling of the story. Deconstructing permits new meanings and understandings to emerge and these can be used in creating new stories and new ways of thinking, feeling, and acting.

Dominant Discourse: The prevailing and conventional way of thinking, understanding, and conversing about a subject or phenomenon in a social group, community, or culture. This way of thinking, conversing and acting about the subject becomes the community's standard and evolves into the traditional presentation, argument, or explanation of that subject. The structured narrative powerfully influences the creation of our realities and worlds. It represents ways of thinking, living, and behaving that are stable and recurring and exert dominance and authority over alternative ways of being. Alternatives are then more likely to be discounted, discredited or suppressed within the community. An example of a dominant discourse within a particular community is the very strong emphasis in the current American culture on individual rights and privilege versus community rights and responsibilities, which are the emphases in some other cultures.

Drift: A never-ending process of living and evolving without a predictable final outcome or direction. The concept has its origins in theoretical biology and evolution and applies to life and social relations. This continuous movement of events, circumstances and context results in continual change for all involved. For example, a hard-working husband who has several young children and a wife who is a full-time mother suddenly dies, and his family discovers his life insurance has expired. The surviving family is suddenly and unexpectedly in serious financial distress. In this case, one unpredictable event cascaded into another and this family, who believed they were financially secure, is set adrift.

Effective Action: Those actions that permit us to produce or achieve a definite or desired result within a defined context of activity or existence. Our functioning, acting or performing in a specific domain leads to the outcome(s) we seek.

Learning Community: A group of people committed to the collaborative exploration of and creation of ideas. Vital components of a learning community include openness to change and an atmosphere of safety that allows for the expression of ideas without judgment. The Institute for Creative Change is a learning community committed to the cooperative and collaborative co-creation of theory and practice relating to change.

Metatheory: A theory about theories. Social construction is a metatheory that addresses how meaning, realities, values, and theories are created relationally among people. Social construction is not a theory of any particular social or clinical phenomenon.

Multiverse: Humberto Maturana used this term to describe the many and diverse beliefs, realities, and world views existing among people at all times. The concept of multiverse strongly challenges the notion of an objective universe and all objective reality and truth. A multiverse permits many different stories and realities to coexist and emphasizes that they are co-constructed among people for the purposes they serve.

Nonlinear: A term borrowed from mathematics to describe a relationship between variables that do not form a straight or predictable line. In social construction, nonlinear emphasizes that we cannot predict the course of events, actions or outcomes in any given human context. It states that A + B does not necessarily equal C.

Past Is Yet to be Defined: This phrase signifies the concept that the past and its meanings can never be described with total accuracy or objectivity. Recall and stories of the past are always being edited and reconstructed. The past is fluid. Memory and remembered stories of the past are only approximations of what happened from any given vantage point at any given time. As time elapses, new ways of telling old stories will evolve, and new descriptions of the past will be created. How many times have scientific explanations for the same phenomena changed through history? People restory the past as the present provides them with new perspectives, experientially and emotionally.

Performance: A term describing the concept that our behavior is analogous to acting. We change our thinking, feeling and behavior based on new scripts and role changes that are co-created in our relationships and changing social contexts.

Perturbations: Those experiences, interactions and disruptions in life that trigger significant change of meaning.

Postmodern: Our current cultural condition, represented by an increasingly post-industrial, information-based and globalized social and economic context. Change is experienced as rapid, chaotic, and unpredictable. Our sense of coherence is undermined by feelings of fragmentation. Our trust in traditional social structures, institutions, beliefs and values is compromised by a world in constant flux with undesirable outcomes, and our confidence in the future has become riddled by uncertainty. This is punctuated by a loss of the modernist belief that knowledge and, especially, scientific knowledge, will bring social and economic progress. Additionally, it recognizes the breakdown of culturally accepted dichotomies such as objective reality and subjective interpretation, self and other, reality and fantasy, fact and fiction, mind and body, and cognition and emotion. These experiences and concepts have arisen over the past century in opposition and contrast to modernist beliefs in individuality, rationality, objectivity, and the existence of knowable and definable truth and reality. These modernist beliefs are replaced by the recognition of the incredible complexity of truth, reality, morality, and ethics that are critical to our social fabric. This appreciation of complexity and variation generates the valuing of context, multiple perspectives, and diverse voices in the construction of these critical beliefs and assumptions.

Reality: The Oxford American Dictionary defines reality as "the quality of being real, resemblance to the original; the real world as distinct from imagination or fantasy." In contrast to this modernist description, social construction defines reality as a perception or perspective that we create relationally within our significant and relevant social groups, including the cultures in which we live. Realities are socially constructed in community and can never be objective. Human beings are not biologically capable of perceiving or defining objective reality, individually or in relationship with others. Our central nervous systems and social systems do not function in this manner.

Reconstruction: After *deconstructing*, previous meanings are edited, deleted, or reorganized and there is a creation of new meaning. These new meanings evolve from conversations and other interactions during and following the process of deconstruction.

Recursive: Having to do with an ongoing process that is applied to or operates on the product of its own operation or functioning. In other terms, a rule or procedure that can be repeatedly applied to the outcome of its previous application as it evolves within the context of those recursive actions. For example, we construct meanings with others by expanding or changing our previous meaning as an outcome of our experiencing another's construction of meaning regarding the shared issue or subject of our discourse. The other person's meaning is similarly expanded or changed as an outcome of our continuing interaction. Their sharing the new meaning with us will similarly expand or change our previous meaning. This recursive process is maintained and meaning continues to evolve for as long as we continue our discourse about the defined issue or subject.

Reflecting Team: The process in which a select group of people reflects together on their observations and perceptions of a target group they have been observing in a structured psychotherapy environment. Tom Anderson, a Norwegian psychiatrist, developed this technique. As part of a therapeutic session with clients, he would leave the session to consult with colleagues who were observing the therapeutic interaction behind a two-way mirror. Dr. Anderson and his colleagues decided that clients could benefit from hearing the reflections made by the observers and he made clients part of the reflecting process, thereby generating the name *reflecting team*. The rules they defined for this process are as follows:

- The client is given permission to listen or not to listen to the reflecting team
- The reflecting team is asked to refrain from giving negative comments and instead is asked to be curious. For example, they might say, "I wonder what would happen if they tried this or that?" and not "I don't understand why they didn't try this or that."
- The reflecting team is asked to look at each other while speaking and not at the client.

Relational Responsibility: A term, originated by Ken Gergen and Sheila McNamee, that defines responsibility as occurring between people rather than within an individual person. This concept is based on the premise that people construct their worlds and themselves in those worlds through their relationships and engagement with others. Relational responsibility holds that relationally responsible actions "lie within the shared attempt to sustain the conditions in which we can join in the construction of meaning and morality." The responsibility for the constructed meanings and resulting behaviors lies within the relationships. As with meaning itself, responsibility for the realities created and the actions that result from these realities exists between people, in their relationships. It does not reside individually inside people. It is mutually created and sustained in every relationship in which people meaningfully relate. It is the moral dimension of all relationships and a necessary element for any relationship or network of relationships to be experienced as safe and nurturing by those participating in those relationships.

Social Construction Theory: A *metatheory* that holds that all claims to knowledge, truth, identity, objectivity, reality, and values are the products of communal relationships and the communal making of meaning. The theory asserts that all human meaning—and therefore all knowledge—arises through the relational generation of those meanings within the context of social interaction. It places relationship at the core of all that we experience as truth, reality, and values. Social construction claims that what we call real and true does not exist or have universal meaning independent of the people and their social context in which these meaning systems have been constructed. Rather, truth, reality, and values are being continuously constructed, deconstructed, and reconstructed within the communities of meaning-making in which we participate. Social construction assumes that our descriptions, explanations, and representations of reality and what we believe evolve from our generative relationships with others and especially, from our interactions in language within those relationships. This provides for a potentially unlimited number of descriptions, explanations, and representations of any given experience or situation. Language cannot map or picture an independent world. How we understand our world is not determined by what is "actually out there." Meaning depends on social and relational process and cannot be perceived or appreciated independent of that process.

Story: The stories we live and tell organize and maintain the meaning systems we have constructed. The concept of story is distinguished from truth and objective reality by punctuating that we create our meanings and realities through our relationships with other people. In striving to make sense of life, people face the task of arranging their experiences of events in sequences across time in such a way as to arrive at a coherent account of themselves and the world in which they live. This account is structured as stories or narratives, both individual and collective. Meaning, reality, knowledge, and values are incorporated into these stories that tell about people and the social organizations they participate in. The collective story provides coherence, credibility and even existence to the organization and the people it represents, whatever that social entity might be.

Storytelling: The process through which we make sense of ourselves and the worlds in which we live, including past, present and future. All people are storytellers. This is how we communicate with others and create meaning and knowledge, including the subjective beliefs, realities and values that guide our actions as people. As human beings, we cannot *not* be storytellers. Constructing our stories and telling our stories is as necessary and as essential as all other primary bodily functions.

Story Dwellers: The concept that people live within the stories and narratives they tell about their lives and their circumstances and the meanings they construct about themselves and the worlds in which they live.

Structural Coupling: A biological process described by Humberto Maturana and Francisco Varela to illustrate what occurs between two or more living systems leading to structural congruence. This term describes an ongoing mutual co-adaptation. Structural coupling is a coordination of actions in the biological world.

Survival of the Fit: A concept introduced by Humberto Maturana and Francisco Varela to describe their interpretation of Darwin's theory of natural selection. They claim that the concept of "the survival of the fittest" is a misrepresentation of natural selection and was not Darwin's intent in his theory. Rather, survival of a species and of an individual of that species depends on maintaining or conserving the evolving adaptation between the species or individual and the environment or, in their terms, maintaining or conserving the fit between the species or individual and its environment. This is not a competitive process between species or between individuals but rather a matter of maintaining an adaptation that provides for continuing existence.

Bibliography

Anderson, Harlene. 1997. *Conversation, language, and possibilities.* New York: Basic Books.

Anderson, Harlene et al. 2001. *The appreciative organization.* Lima, OH: Taos Institute Publishing.

Bateson, Catherine. 1994. *Peripheral visions: Learning along the way.* New York: Harper Collins.

Bateson, Gregory. 1979. *Mind and nature: A necessary unity.* New York: E.P. Dutton.

Bruner, Jerome. 1990. *Acts of meaning.* Cambridge, MA: Harvard University Press.

Cooperrider, David L. and Diana Whitney. 1999. *Collaborating for change: Appreciative inquiry.* San Francisco: Barrett-Koehler.

Cooperrider, David L. et al, eds. 1999. *Appreciative inquiry: Rethinking human organization toward a positive theory of change.* Champaign, IL: Stipes Publishing.

DeBono, Edward. 1991. *Serious creativity.* New York: Harper Collins.

Frank, Arthur W. 1995. *The wounded storyteller.* Chicago: The University of Chicago Press.

Gergen, Kenneth J. 1991. *The saturated self.* New York: Basic Books.

Gergen, Kenneth J. 1994. *Toward transformation in social knowledge.* 2nd ed. Thousand Oaks, CA: Sage Publications.

Gergen, Kenneth J. 1994. *Realities and relationships: Soundings in social construction.* Cambridge, MA: Harvard University Press.

Gergen, Kenneth J. 1999. *An invitation to social construction.* Thousand Oaks, CA: Sage Publications.

Gergen, Kenneth J. 2002. *Social construction in context.* Thousand Oaks, CA: Sage Publications, Inc.

Gergen, Mary and Sara N. Davis, eds. 1997. *Toward a new psychology of gender.* New York: Routledge.

Gergen, Mary. 2001. *Feminist reconstructions in psychology.* Thousand Oaks, CA: Sage Publications.

Gergen, Mary and Gergen, Kenneth J. 2002. *Social construction: A reader.* Thousand Oaks, CA: Sage Publications.

Gleick, James. 1987. *Chaos: Making a new science.* New York: Viking Penguin Inc.

Gregory, Bruce 1988. *Inventing reality: Physics as language.* New York: John Wiley & Sons, Inc.

Harre, Rom and Grant Gillett. 1994. *The discursive mind.* Thousand Oaks, CA: Sage Publications.

Harre, Rom and W. Gerrod Parrott 1996. *The emotions.* Thousand Oaks, CA: Sage Publications.

Holtzman, Lois and John Morss, eds. 2000. *Postmodern psychologies, societal practice, and political life.* New York: Routledge.

Johnson, Allan G. 2001. *Privilege, power, and difference*. New York: McGraw-Hill.

Kotter, John P. 1996. *Leading change*. Boston, MA: Harvard Business School Press.

Kvale, Steinar. 1992. *Psychology and postmodernism*. London: Sage Publications.

Maturana, Humberto and Francisco J. Varela. 1992. *The tree of knowledge: The biological roots of human understanding*. Revised ed. Boston: Shambhala Publications.

McNamee, Sheila and Kenneth J. Gergen, eds. 1992. *Therapy as social construction*. Thousand Oaks, CA: Sage Publications.

McNamee, Sheila and Kenneth J. Gergen. 1999. *Relational responsibility: Resources for sustaining dialogue*. Thousand Oaks, CA: Sage Publications.

Middleton, David and Derek Edwards. 1990. *Collective remembering*. Thousand Oaks, CA: Sage Publications.

Prigogine, Ilya and Isabelle Stengers. 1984. *Order out of chaos*. New York: Bantam Books.

Ricketts, Miriam W. and James E. Willis. 2001. *Experience AI: A practitioner's guide to integrating appreciative inquiry with experiential learning*. Lima, OH: Taos Institute Publishing.

Schiller, Marjorie, Bea Mah Holland, and Deanna Riley. 2001. *Appreciative leaders: In the eye of the beholder*. Lima, OH: Taos Institute Publishing.

Schrage, Michael. 1990. *Shared Minds*. New York: Random House.

Semin, Gun R. and Kenneth J. Gergen. 1990. *Everyday understanding: Social and scientific implications*. Thousand Oaks, CA: Sage Publications.

Shotter, John and Kenneth J. Gergen. 1990. *Texts of identity*. Thousand Oaks, CA: Sage Publications.

Shotter, John. 1993. *Conversational realities*. Thousand Oaks, CA: Sage Publications.

Shotter, John. 1993. *Cultural politics of everyday life*. Toronto: University of Toronto Press.

Simons, Herbert W. 1989. *Rhetoric in the human sciences*. Thousand Oaks, CA: Sage Publications.

Srivastra, Suresh and David L. Cooperrider. 1998. *Organizational wisdom and executive courage*. San Francisco: New Lexington Press.

Srivastra, Suresh and David L. Cooperrider. 1999. *Appreciative management and leadership: The power of positive thought and action in organizations*. Revised ed. San Francisco: Jossey-Bass.

Stone, Douglas, Bruce Patton, and Sheila Heen. 1999. *Difficult conversations*. New York: Viking.

Vaill, Peter B. 1996. *Learning as a way of being*. San Francisco: Jossey-Bass.

Varela, Francisco J., Evan T. Thompson, and Eleanor Rosh. 1993. *The embodied mind: Cognitive science and human experience*. Cambridge, MA: The MIT Press.

Waldrop, M. Mitchell. 1992. *Complexity: The emerging science at the edge of order and chaos*. New York: Simon & Schuster.

Weick, Karl. 1995. *Sensemaking in organizations*. Thousand Oaks, CA: Sage
Publications.

Wheatley, Margaret J. and Myron Kellner-Rogers. 1996. *A simpler way*. San Francisco:
Berrett-Koehler Publishers.

Whitney, Diana and Amanda Trosten-Bloom. 2002. *The power of appreciative inquiry*.
San Francisco: Barrett-Koehler.

Winograd, Terry and Fernando Flores. 1992. *Understanding Computers and Cognition*.
Boston: Addison Wesley.

About the Authors

Robert Cottor, M.D., is a family and organizational psychiatrist in private practice. He received his medical and child psychiatric training at the University of Minnesota and practiced as a child and adolescent psychiatrist in the public sector in Minnesota and in California before moving to Arizona in 1971. In his practice Bob focuses on individual, couple, family and business relationships; family wealth issues; the creation of positive aging; family business consulting; and divorce and child custody issues. He has been a leader in marriage and family therapy in Arizona since arriving in Scottsdale over 30 years ago. Bob received a special citation for Outstanding Contributions to the Field from the Arizona Association of Marriage and Family Therapy in 1992. He and his wife, Sharon Cottor, L.C.S.W., founded the Institute for Creative Change in 1980 as the first community program in Arizona that provided family therapy training for practicing mental health professionals. They have been pioneers in applying relational, appreciative, and social constructionist concepts and methods to the everyday practices of clinicians, educators, and business consultants. Bob has been a member of the Taos Institute community since its beginning and was recently chosen to serve on the Board of the Taos Institute.

Alan Asher, M.C., L.M.F.T., L.P.C., is a marriage and family therapist in private practice. He is a clinical member of the American Association for Marriage and Family Therapy and is currently president-elect of the Arizona Division. He has been associated with the Institute for Creative Change since its early years and has been co-anchor of the Learning Lab Series for many years. Alan finds social construction to be a fascinating tool for keeping the mind open to possibility. He immersed himself in the different cultural construct as a Peace Corps volunteer in Nepal. Alan's undergraduate degree is in English and creative writing from the University of Arizona.

Judith A. Levin, M.S., R.N., C.S., N.P., is a nurse practitioner and therapist in private practice. She is a social constructionist therapist participating in the co-creation of effective change with her clients. Judith is a faculty member of the Institute for Creative

Change and has contributed to the Institute's website and to the development and facilitation of Learning Labs, Salons and conferences internationally. Her experiences in the Institute for Creative Change have enriched and enhanced her service to the refugee community, her providing of health care for communities in need, and her own personal life.

Cindy Caplan Weiser, M.S.W., A.C.S.W., L.C.S.W., has been in private practice since 1985 and has been on the faculty of the Institute for Creative Change since 1994. She brings concepts of social construction thinking to individuals, couples, and families who look to shift from narrow to generative ways of thinking, feeling, and doing. Cindy has co-facilitated conferences and workshops focused on creative change and was the co-anchor of the Learning Labs from 1996 to 2000. Her commitment to community service offers her a context to bring innovative ideas to organizations and committees involved in projects with the goals of service and change.